EMPIRICAL TRUTHS AND
CRITICAL FICTIONS

Empirical Truths and Critical Fictions

LOCKE, WORDSWORTH, KANT, FREUD

Cathy Caruth

The Johns Hopkins University Press
Baltimore

© 1991 The Johns Hopkins University Press
All rights reserved. Published 1991
Printed in the United States of America

Johns Hopkins Paperback edition, 2009
9 8 7 6 5 4 3 2 1

The Johns Hopkins University Press
2715 North Charles Street
Baltimore, Maryland 21218-4363
www.press.jhu.edu

*The Library of Congress has catalogued the hardcover edition of
this book as follows:*

Caruth, Cathy, 1955–
    Empirical truths and critical fictions : Locke, Wordsworth,
Kant, Freud / Cathy Caruth.
        p.   cm.
    ISBN 0-8018-4080-5 (alk. paper)
    1. Literature—History and criticism.   2. Empiricism.
3. Locke, John 1632–1704—Influences.   4. Kant, Immanuel
1724–1804.   5. Freud, Sigmund 1856–1939.   6. Wordsworth,
William 1770–1850—Criticism and interpretation.   I. Title.
PN81.C38   1991
146'.44—dc20   90-39243
                                                      CIP

ISBN 13: 978-0-8018-9269-1
ISBN 10: 0-8018-9269-4

CONTENTS

PREFACE

The present study proposes to explore the enigma of experience and the significance of the recurring questions of empiricism in John Locke's *Essay Concerning Human Understanding* (1690), William Wordsworth's *Prelude* (1805), Immanuel Kant's *Prolegomena to Any Future Metaphysics* (1783) and *Metaphysical Foundations of Natural Science* (1786), and Sigmund Freud's *Civilization and Its Discontents* (1930). These works, in their variety, might nonetheless essentially all be defined as studies in self-knowledge, or attempts by thought to turn upon itself. The form that self-reflection takes differs in each case, whether it be the philosophical reflection on knowledge (Locke and Kant), the narrative of the poetic spirit (Wordsworth), or the analysis of the psyche (Freud). But in the movement of their different arguments, each of these texts reproduces a surprisingly similar scene: the scene of the encounter between a parent and a child, an encounter that uncannily takes place not as an exchange among the living, but as a relation to the dead, as a scene of mourning or of murder, and of the confrontation between a parent and a dead child, or between a child and a dead parent.

The face-to-face meeting of parent and child might easily be read, in Enlightenment as well as in Romantic texts, as a representation of the origins, or the conditions, of self-knowledge, of the mind facing itself. But what are these texts trying to tell us if, at the very origin, one of these figures is already dead, already a part of the past? How can there be, at the origin, already a memory? What kind of a remembering can be thus dramatized as being, in itself, an original beginning? And what, then, is a self-knowledge that begins as, or reflects, this "memory," something that is not fully and completely knowledge? It is only by addressing these recurring questions, I would suggest, that we can begin to review and to rethink both the significance of the notion of experience and the complexity of the insistence of empiricism in these traditions.

Taking as a starting point Locke's empirical philosophy as one influential source of the vocabulary of experience, this book sketches out the steps and the consequences of a reading that no longer takes this vocabulary at face value—a reading that begins, indeed, by treating Locke himself not simply as a philosophical doctrine but also as a narrative in which "experience" plays an unexpected and uncanny role. The transformations of this narrative in later texts will then confirm the suggestion that experience is, in effect, less a concept (over which the later doctrines struggle) than a singular encounter—a point of convergence or divergence—between literature and philosophy.

In reflecting thus implicitly on the connections between literature, philosophy, and psychoanalytic inquiry, and in moving, in each chapter, from a conceptual and general opening and from the theoretical framework of some central questions to the singularity of a specific text and to the particular resistance of specific stories to abstraction, the present study also asks persistently what is the place, the function, the uniqueness of *position* of the literary text and of literary criticism. In each of the chapters that follow, literary theory puts into question traditional notions of period and genre. It does not, however, simply mourn the loss of these notions, nor reassert the individuality of the texts differentiated by them, but rather, like the mad, melancholic mother evoked by Locke, endlessly repeats the question of their difference.

ACKNOWLEDGMENTS

The original project of this book was motivated by the teaching of the late Paul de Man. I am grateful to Geoffrey Hartman for his critical attention and comments on the entire manuscript, and to other teachers and colleagues who have discussed and read all or parts of the manuscript, and who have provided the intellectual stimulation for my work: Harold Bloom, J. Hillis Miller, Andrzej Warminski, Cynthia Chase, Shoshana Felman, Kevin Newmark, Thomas Greene, and David Marshall. I would like to give special thanks to the friends and colleagues who provided both crucial insights and support and without whose advice the completion of this work would not have been possible: David Guenther (whose creative explanations of Newtonian physics contributed to my understanding of the problems faced by Kantian philosophy), Dolora Wojciehowski, and Thomas McCall. I received helpful suggestions as well from Thomas Keenan, Jill Robbins, Jonathan Culler, Timothy Bahti, Ian Balfour, Deborah Esch, and Roger Blood. I am also grateful to Marie Blanchard for her sensitive copyediting of the manuscript, to Michael Shae for careful preparation of the index, and to Kimberly Johnson for her help with the proofs. Finally, I would like to thank my family for their unfailing support and my mother, in addition, for her perceptive advice.

Earlier versions of Chapters Two, Three, and Four appeared in *MLN* 100:5 (1985), *Yale French Studies* 74 (1988), and *PsychCritique* 2:3 (1987), respectively. The completion of the manuscript was funded in part by grants from the Mrs. Giles Whiting Foundation and from the A. Whitney Griswold Fund.

EMPIRICAL TRUTHS
AND CRITICAL FICTIONS

1

THE FACE OF EXPERIENCE

 Locke's *Essay Concerning Human Understanding* stands in a peculiar relation to the tradition that it founded. On the one hand, the school known as associationism, represented most prominently by David Hartley, depended on Locke's assertion that ideas are derived from experience. The principle by which these ideas were said to be governed, moreover, was designated by a phrase lifted out of the fourth edition of Locke's *Essay,* "the association of ideas." On the other hand, the use of *association* to name a central principle of rational thought altered the meaning it had in Locke's work, in which it referred to a thought process subversive of normal reasoning and described as a "madness." While Locke assumed, like the later associationists, that reason normally operates by combining simple ideas according to their "natural connections," he reserved the name "association" for the formation of "accidental" connections that unconsciously influence the reasoning process. In transferring the name to "rational" thought processes, the eighteenth-century empiricists effectively eliminated the phenomenon that, in Locke, had raised serious questions about the principles established in the rest of the *Essay.* The very term that introduced a counterpoint in Locke's analysis of reason came to stand for a type of empiricism known for its simple, "mechanistic" form of explanation.

Despite the sporadic recognition of this anomaly in the history of British philosophy, it has received little sustained attention.[1] "Association of ideas" is itself associated, most frequently, with the eighteenth-century empiricists, for whom Locke is generally understood to be the starting point.[2] The implications of such an approach are perhaps most apparent in studies of English Romanticism, which have often attempted to define the period in relation to the empirical tradition. Whether this relation is seen as essentially negative, or positive, or as a working-through and transcendence of empiricism by Romantic texts, the pattern remains fundamentally the same: whatever the individual doctrinal differences, empiricism is characterized as a general philosophical approach exemplified variously by Locke, Hartley, Erasmus Darwin, and others, to which Romanticism is a more or less complex response.[3] A number of interpretations of English Romantic texts depend on an approach to empiricism which neglects the complexities of individual arguments as well as the peculiarities of the tradition as a whole.

The consequences of this view of empirical philosophy are most apparent in works that interpret Romantic texts in terms of a vocabulary of experience. The concept of experience, which is as varied as it is central to empirical philosophies, tends to be lifted uncritically from the context of these arguments and used as a framework in which to understand the complex issues of Romantic poetry. The problems of literary convention, diction, and figuration are then neglected for the poem's reference to a world of passion, thought, and other aspects of experience.[4] This occurs particularly around the terminology of sensation. Empirical arguments concerning sensation are usually read literally, presumably because the texts are "philosophical," and insist on the literal status of their own language, and because they claim with this authority that sensation is a basic unit of experience. The referential status of the language of sensation thus tends to overcome the often peculiar way these terms are actually used in various arguments, which employ their own conventional and figurative devices. The empiricist's claim to refer to an empirical world is taken, that is, at face value, and the power of this reference affects the reading of certain terms even in the more explicitly figurative contexts of Romantic poetry. In the "nature poetry" of Wordsworth, for example, the ultimate reference of words such as *perception* and *eye* is usually read in terms of a model of physiological experience—even when the claims made *about* such experience are said to differ radically from the claims of the empiricists. Thus when Wordsworth is said to make creative thought the basis of perception, in opposition to certain empirical doctrines, the term *perception* is still read in both cases on the basis of its reference to a physiological experience.[5] Regardless of the differences said to exist between what the texts say *about* experience, the general notion of "experience" as an interpretive framework remains within the context of a literal and generalized reading of empirical philosophy. A more careful consideration of the actual complexities of these philosophical texts raises serious questions about the adequacy of this approach. As we shall see, the first question Locke's *Essay* raises is the way in which the vocabulary of experience is to be interpreted.

A closely related assumption that affects the reading of Romantic texts is that empiricism suffers from the same weakness for which Coleridge denigrated the concept of association, that is, that it "leaves itself unexplained."[6] This point of view is generally contained within the larger categorization of empiricism as an uncritical or non-speculative philosophical tradition. Unlike the self-brooding Germans, said to account for every moment of their own speculations, the empiricists are deemed willing to give all the credit to the sensory world and to forget the necessarily active nature of their own thinking. English Romantic poetry, occasionally read in conjunction with the work of Germans such as Hegel, has always seemed to transcend this un-self-consciousness and to make its own creative act a central focus. If we reread a text such as Locke's *Essay,* however, we discover, particularly in sections such as the chapter on association, that it establishes its own mode of self-interpretation. This "self-accounting" in Locke is not thematized; it has no place in the explicit *doctrine* of his *Essay*. Rather its strategies require an interpretive method that reads beyond doctrine and pays close attention to the way in which the argument is presented. The very obliqueness of this self-accounting in fact frees us from a literal understanding of "sensation" and "reflection," or perception and thought, and calls for a way of talking about empirical philosophies not just as doctrines but as texts. With *this* empiricism as a starting point, we might consider new ways of reading the self-meditations of Romantic texts as well, and of talking about the difference between those self-accountings that are thematic, and form a "doctrine," and those more indirect ways in which Romantic texts tell about themselves. A rereading of empiricism, in other words, can open up our ideas of self-understanding insofar as it is an essential part of the interpretive vocabulary of Romantic poetry.

The implications of a reinterpretation of empirical arguments thus extend beyond the understanding of any individual empirical philosopher. Such a project can teach us to reconsider the framework in which we read English Romantic poetry, particularly as it is determined by a vocabulary of experience. This will affect not only what we learn from the texts of the empiricists and the Romantics, but also how we define them in relation to each other: how we establish the genres of "philosophy" and "poetry," and how we define the English "empirical" and Romantic traditions. Locke's *Essay*, because of its important as well as complex position in these traditions, provides a good starting point for this project.

Observing the Limits

The "empirical" nature of Locke's *Essay* can be understood only in the context of its larger philosophical aims. Locke defines his work as a project of self-understanding, the means by which reason can attain full certainty of itself. The certainty of self-knowledge is described as a self-enclosed and luminous territory:

> I thought that the first Step towards satisfying several Enquiries, the Mind of Man was very apt to run into, was, to take a Survey of our own Understandings, examine our own Powers, and see to what Things they were adapted . . . Were the Capacities of our Understandings well considered, the Extent of our Knowledge once discovered, and the Horizon found, which sets the Bounds between the enlightned and dark Parts of Things: . . . Men would perhaps with less scruple acquiesce in the avow'd Ignorance of the one, and imploy their Thoughts and Discourse, with more Advantage and Satisfaction in the other. (Introduction)[7]

This is an early statement of an important principle in Enlightenment philosophy, the acknowledgment of the limits of understanding.[8] Its power as a philosophical principle (rather than as an article of faith) is that it makes possible the self-sufficiency of reason in its attempt to establish its own certainty. As such, it serves a rhetorical function that turns it into something of a philosophical humility topos: its apparent subject, the limitation of reason, really tells of a new and unbounded power of reason over its own territory. What we are told of here is less the setting of bounds than the surveying of a new land discovered as reason looks away from the heavens and turns back toward itself. Such a land is in the complete possession of reason, since it is itself nothing other than reason. Rational certainty, the general philosophical goal of the *Essay*, is thus to be founded on a kind of self-understanding—the knowledge of the extent and limits of knowledge. Locke's project is to establish the certainty of this self-knowledge, which is represented as a kind of self-reflection in an enclosed and lighted realm.

The means by which such certainty is said to be possible is

what characterizes the *Essay* as an "empirical" argument. The word *empirical* comes from the Greek word for experience, and it is the emphasis that Locke placed on experience as the guarantor of rational certainty that earned him the label of an empirical philosopher.[9] In the opening lines of the *Essay*, understanding becomes comprehensible to itself in an experience very much like that of visual perception:

> The Understanding, like the Eye, whilst it makes us see, and perceive all other Things, takes no notice of it self: And it requires Art and Pains to set it at a distance, and make it its own Object. But . . . sure I am, that all the Light we can let in upon our own Minds . . . will . . . bring us great Advantage. (Introduction)

The figure of understanding as an eye is a common philosophical motif, but in this case the self-containment and self-perception of the "eye" serve specifically to emphasize the natural rather than divine nature of the light: this is not revelation but rational experience. In this passage as well as in the rest of the *Essay*, the analogy between physical and mental observation as comparable forms of experience is precisely what establishes the certainty of self-knowledge: the understanding can see itself as clearly as the sensory eye sees its objects. And this analogy implies as well that the *Essay* is the extension of such self-observation. The argument for self-certainty depends first of all on the claim that self-knowledge is structured like perception.[10]

This central principle gives rise to a second significant feature of the argument, the claim that reason observes itself most thoroughly by observing the origins of its ideas, origins that are located in empirical space and time. Locke in large part defines his work in response to the doctrine of innate ideas, which held that certain concepts and propositions are inherent in the human mind at birth.[11] "What is wrong with this doctrine, according to Locke, is that it puts the origins of ideas in the wrong place, a place that is inaccessible to reason. The *Essay* essentially relocates these origins from an extra-experiential realm (before and outside of reason) to a place that is completely available to rational inspection:

> Let us then suppose the Mind to be, as we say, white Paper, void of all Characters, without any *Ideas;* How comes it to be furnished? Whence comes it by that vast store, which the busy and boundless Fancy of Man has painted on it, with an almost endless variety? Whence has it all the materials of Reason and Knowledge? To this I answer, in one word, From *Experience . . . Our Observation employ'd either about external, sensible Objects; or about the internal Operations of our Minds, perceived and reflected on by our selves, is that, which supplies our Understandings with all the materials of thinking.* These two are the Fountains of Knowledge, from whence all the *Ideas* we have, or can naturally have, do spring. (II.1.2)

This passage suggests that understanding is completely available to itself because its ideas come from places within its experience: from the external world perceived in visual observation (or by means of "sensation") and the internal world perceived in mental observation (or by means of "reflection").[12] For ideas to come "from experience" means that they can be "observed," either through the eye or through its analogue, the understanding. The argument can be considered empirical because it handles the question concerning the nature of ideas in terms of the notion of places; or more generally because it conceives of the knowledge of knowledge as the tracing of "fountains," an activity modeled on visual perception. The notion of "experience" as a double origination in sensation and reflection is thus a correlate of the analogy between eye and understanding. Both notions ensure that reflection, or self-knowledge, will be as open to inspection as sensation, or knowledge of the world. The principles of a dual "eye" and of two sources of ideas base the certainty of self-understanding on empirical, or as Locke calls it, "historical" description.

The importance of these two principles in Locke is evidenced by the history of Locke interpretation. Locke's "empiricism" has been characterized most often in terms of the sort of "observation" he is said to attribute to the mind, and by the emphasis he is said to place on one or the other of the two origins. These interpretations, however, have also revealed some difficulties in the apparent simplicity of Locke's argument. Characterizations of Locke's empiricism have struggled especially with the dual-structured "observation"; the criterion for the differentiation of sensation and reflection has shifted from the distinction between mechanism and mind, to the opposition between passivity and activity. In this connection there has also been some uncertainty in the criteria by which Locke is judged. A brief look at two instances will help focus the problem.

The first viewpoint is offered by a modern literary critic, who assesses Locke's role in the eighteenth-century representation of mind.[13] Locke, as part of a "sensationist tradition" beginning with Hobbes, is said to have been primarily responsible for passing this tradition on to later writers:

> John Locke—who more than any other philosopher established the stereotype for the popular view of the mind in the eighteenth century—was able to levy upon a long tradition of ready-made parallels in giving definition to his view of the mind in perception as a passive receiver for images presented ready-formed from without.[14]

The emphasis in this summary is twofold: on the one hand it focuses on Locke's source of ideas in sensation as a physiological, perceptual activity, and on the other it describes the passivity of a "mind" which is separate from and subjugated to this mechanism. The use of "perception" suggests a physiological model, while the notion of "passivity" introduces a volitional element. The distinction between a mind which is itself only sensation and a mind which is passively subjugated to sensation is easy to miss, and the two points have often been confused. Thus, the sensationist interpretation of Locke often implies, first of all, an entirely "materialistic" model of mind, a mechanism in which corpuscular ideas obey mechanical laws. At the same time, this interpretation may refer to the "passivity" of Locke's model of mind with connotations of a relation between two subjects, in which one is submitted to the other (a different sort of "obeying laws"). Thus the "mechanistic" model is not judged as insufficient as an explanation, or incorrect as a fact, but as pessimistic about the human mind or as having little faith in it. This response implies an interpretation of the relation between sensation and mind as the story of a struggle of weak and strong rather than as an argument or explanation. The focus on the apparent mechanicity of mind is framed as a response to a story.[15]

The other pole of interpretation opposes itself to the first by focusing on the role of reflection in the *Essay*. A modern psychologist emphasizes Locke's assertion of such an "origin" as what distinguishes his empiricism from mere sensationism:[16]

> According to Locke, all ideas come from sensations . . . So we see that his point of departure is sensualistic. But Locke, unlike Hobbes, did not stop at sensualism; he considered also another basic activity of the soul, reflection. In place of the anemic Hobbesian empiricism founded merely on sensation, here psychic activity is twofold: reflection absorbs the material supplied by sensation. Reflection is the proper activity of the mind . . . it changes the sensory data . . . Mere sensualism is transformed into empiricism.[17]

This interpretation, like the other, seems at first to be an assessment of the explanatory power of Locke's argument. Sensation is interpreted as a physiological mechanism, and reflection is opposed to it as a more sufficient means of explaining the functions "proper" to the mind. But the description of Hobbesian empiricism as "anemic" and the repetition of the adjective "mere" in front of "sensualism" suggest that what is "proper" about reflection as an activity of the mind is, precisely, that it is an activity: it is not weak, anemic, or passive like sensation. The "transformation" of sensualism into empiricism thus reads more like the climax of a story, the victory of reflection over sensation, than a statement of fact. In spite of its differences from the first interpretation concerning *what* Locke says, this interpretation also reads Locke similarly in terms of the *way* he says it, that is, as a story.

The similarity of these responses suggests that the terms by which we are to characterize Locke's empiricism cannot simply be the doctrine he espouses, but the way in which this doctrine presents itself as a narrative. The difference between the doctrine and the form in which it is presented is apparent already in the passage, quoted above, on the origins of ideas. In asking about the origins of the "materials of Reason and Knowledge," Locke finds the answer, as he says, "in one word, From Experience." *Experience* is the "one word" by which understanding can solve its uncertainties about itself; it is the fully observable place in which the mind can perceive its own operation. The "single term" represents the unity and self-enclosure of the mind as knower and object of knowledge, by representing both as an aspect of perception, that is, as empirical eye and empirical object. But if *experience* is the "one word" which establishes understanding's self-certainty, the passage in fact uses two words, "*From* Experience," to *tell* of this certainty. In these two words we have the beginning of a narrative that takes, throughout the *Essay,* a somewhat darker turn, and suggests something rather different from the transparency of an observation. When understanding observes itself, we find, it tells a story that follows laws very different from those of perception. Our reinterpretation of Locke, our attempt to read the *Essay* as a complex narrative as well as a doctrine, will thus begin with an examination of the argument concerning the origins of ideas, and the curious story that arises within it.

Sensation and Reflection

In the introductory remarks on understanding, as we have seen, Locke establishes physical perception as a model for the way in which understanding comes to know itself. This implies that the *Essay's* analysis of knowledge, in regard to both sensation and reflection, will have the clarity of observation. In the extended treatment of sensation, however, the discussion turns toward a notion of passivity not entirely consonant with the empirical model:

> In this Part, the *Understanding* is meerly *passive* . . . For the Objects of our Senses, do, many of them, obtrude their particular *Ideas* upon our minds, whether we will or no . . . As the Bodies that surround us, do diversly affect our Organs, the mind is forced to receive the Impressions; and cannot avoid the Perception of those *Ideas* that are annexed to them. (II.1.25)

Sensation is defined here as the passive reception by the mind of sensory impressions originating in the external world. This seems to be a fairly straightforward description, yet the characterization of the understanding as passive functions in several distinctly different ways. Passivity is in the first place associated with what seems to be an observation concerning the mechanical operation of the sense organs: their function depends on the physical state of the body rather than on conscious intention. In this sense *passive* is a synonym for *mechanical*. On the other hand, the distinction between "bodies" that "affect our organs" and the "mind" which is "forced to receive the impressions" attributes passivity to a more elusive agent, the mind or understanding, which is subjugated to the sense organs and what enters them as to a group of strangers. Used in this way passivity is an attribute of willing agents. Both of these connotations can be read in the word *as*, which implies first of all a causal relation between the affection of the organs and the reception by the mind, and thus tends toward a physiological understanding of the latter—and also suggests an analogical relation between organs and mind, in which the mind becomes personified as that which "sees" along with the eye. The characterization of ideas as "annexed" to impressions reiterates this distinction, the full ambiguity of which falls on the word *receive*. Reception as a physical concept is juxtaposed, here, with the notion of a "forced" activity, an onslaught of unwelcome guests. The description of sensation as an object of observation shifts to a narration of sensation as the mind's entrapment.

Several chapters further into the *Essay*, the connotations of "reception" are clearly articulated in a more self-conscious use of a figurative analogy. Attempting to prove the dependence of certain "simple ideas" on sensation, Locke turns to the negative evidence of bodily injury:

> If these Organs, or the Nerves which are the Conduits, to convey [noises, tastes, smells, etc.] from without to their Audience in the Brain, the mind's Presence-room (as I may so call it) are any of them so disordered, as not to perform their Functions, they have no Postern to be admitted by; no other way to bring themselves into view, and be perceived by the Understanding. (II.3.1)

The distinction here between the "mind" and sensation is clearly not conceptual but dramatic, a power relation between acting agents. As one critic, Ernest Tuveson, notes of the passage, the figure of the "presence-room," familiar to Locke as the spokesman of the first Lord Shaftesbury, turns the understanding into a "judge, seated majestically within his presence-room, where ideas are ushered in for disposal." "Like a ruler," Tuveson says of this judge, "he is powerful and autonomous, but depends absolutely on his retainers."[18] The passivity of the understanding is thus defined in terms of human political relations; what seems at first a straightforward observation of sensory mechanisms becomes more like an anxious story of a precariously governed state.

The ambiguous function of "reception" is focused in this passage on the concept of motion. In the "materialist" philosophies of earlier writers, particularly Hobbes, it is the concept of motion which governs the description of the mind; in accordance with a Newtonian model, body and mind are united by "motions" obedient to mechanical laws (a concept which reappears, more complexly, in Hartley's theory of vibrations).[19]

When Locke speaks of sensations as beginning with "organs," and being "conveyed" by "nerves" to the "brain," he seems to use a purely materialist terminology describing sensation as the physical propagation of motion from one organ to another. But the introduction of the term *audience* in the phrase "audience in the brain" changes the literal language of motion, which refers to the physical world, to a figurative language: the movement from outside-the-senses to inside-the-brain becomes the movement from outside-the-presence-room to inside-the-presence-room, with further connotations of a "movement" from "outside" to "inside" the sphere of the ruler.[20] The change from literal to figurative passage rests, moreover, on the word *for* passage, the word *convey*. While "conveying" from organ to brain would be a simple movement from one physical location to another, conveying from organ to mind marks a passage from a physical to a nonphysical realm, and hence the word itself can no longer be understood in physical terms. In the word *convey*, sensation changes from a literal to a figurative motion, and the argument changes from a description to a narrative. One of the first problems Locke's argument poses is thus how to interpret the language of sensation, and specifically the terminology of motion. Both the figurative meaning of motion and the narrative dimensions of the description suggest that the discussion of sensation operates on principles less like a "natural philosophy" than a literary text.[21]

The figurative nature of motion in the *Essay*—the fact that words for motion do not simply refer to the empirical world—is foregrounded by the alternation between a terminology of motion, as "conveying," with one of light as "imprinting on the mind." These terms are not ordered in a physical sequence (as a motion of impulses leading to an imprinting) but substitute directly for one another. Their interchangeability is particularly evident when the imprinting-metaphor takes on the attributes of aggressivity otherwise associated with motion inward:

All that are born into the World being surrounded with Bodies, that perpetually and diversly affect them, variety of Ideas, whether care be taken of it or no, are imprinted on the Minds of Children. *Light*, and *Colours*, are busie at hand every where, when the Eye is but open; *Sounds*, and some *tangible Qualities* fail not to solicite their proper Senses, and force an entrance to the Mind. (II.1.6)

Here, again, the concern with an "entrance to the Mind," one moreover that is "forced," translates the description of a physical process into a narrative. "Imprinting," like "conveying," does not simply refer to a physiological process, but is narrated as an anxiety-ridden story in which the empirical world *solicits* or seduces and then forces itself upon an unsuspecting mind. This means that the choice of the terminology of motion and light is not self-evidently based on experimental evidence— connected for example with Locke's medical experience and his forays into Newtonian physics and optics—but may be governed by laws more closely linked to the figurative universe of the text. Motion and light are not, after all, described here *as* physical sensations or "simple ideas," but as contributing to the *cause* of them. Interestingly, it is motion and light which, in a later book, become prime examples of those "simple ideas" known only by sensation;[22] here, however, their importance is in their incorporation into the *genesis* of simple ideas of sensation. They order the causal relation between external object and internal idea in a sequence which *seems* visible to the eye (as motion or light) even though its central core is not necessarily understandable in these terms. The figurative nature of this pseudogenesis becomes evident in the characterization of sounds and other qualities as "soliciting": the displacement of self-understanding into observed motion and then causal connection finally becomes a drama of influence.

It is not, therefore, as a description of motion, nor as an explanation of causes, but as a story of influence-relations that the argument concerning sensation finally presents itself.[23] In the description of "experience" as the locus of understanding's perceptual self-enclosure, a narrative emerges which is concerned, precisely, with the uncontrolled disruption of enclosed spaces. It is in this narrative of spatial disruption that we can begin to trace a possible disruption of the mind's self-contemplation in the *Essay*.

Once we are aware of the problems raised by the argument concerning sensation, the discussion of reflection becomes more interesting for the similarities in its figurations than for the differences in its "object." Moreover, since the *Essay* is itself represented as a mode of self-reflection, its reflection *on* reflection will have priority as the most certain and self-conscious moment of self-understanding. When we turn to these passages, we find that the discussion centers on the analogy with which the *Essay* opens, the similarity of visual perception and understanding:

> The other Fountain, from which Experience furnisheth the Understanding with *Ideas,* is the *Perception of the Operations of our own Minds* within us, as it is employ'd about the Ideas it has got; which Operations, when the Soul comes to reflect on, and consider, do furnish the Understanding with another set of *Ideas,* which could not be had from things without: and such are, *Perception, Thinking, Doubting, Believing, Reasoning, Knowing, Willing,* and all the different actings of our own Minds; which we being conscious of, and observing in our selves, do from these receive into our Understandings, as distinct *Ideas,* as we do from Bodies affecting our Senses. This Source of *Ideas,* every Man has wholly in himself: And though it be not Sense, as having nothing to do with external Objects; yet it is very like it, and might properly enough be call'd internal Sense. (II.1.4)

The emphasis on reflection as a source (rather than as an act) is the most significant feature of the analogy with sensation: it distinguishes between physical perception and self-knowledge on the basis of an empirical distinction, that of inside and outside. Thus the difference between the activities of reflection and sensation is marked only by the adjective "internal": reflection differs from sensation in the location of the objects that it observes rather than in the nature of the act of observing. In this way the act of reflection itself becomes structured like the empirical relation between eye and object, rather than as a dialectical relation of pure self-reflexivity: what it observes is not precisely its own activity of reflecting, but other mental activities such as "thinking," "believing," and so on.[24] The foundation of sensation as an empirical relation between mind, eye, and object thus extends to reflection as well, the structure of which keeps it from spiraling off into the uncertainties of dialectical self-questioning. This also, retrospectively, assures the certainty of the *Essay*'s account of sensation, since the entire work is itself in the reflective mode. Because reflection is structured like sensation, the *Essay*'s account of both sensation and reflection will have the phenomenal certainty of visual perception.[25]

It is not surprising, considering the complications in the representation of sensation, that the analogy by which reflection is defined rapidly loses its empirical force. Reflection, since it is not simply a self-reflexive act, is structured as a relation between an observer and its object. The word *understanding* in the passage above, as a locus separate from the "fountain" of reflection, designates a receptacle or agent of reception which "receives" and is "furnished" with its "objects." While these ideas, the various activities of thought, are active powers of the mind, reflection remains passive. The reflective mind is thus separated from itself much as the sensing mind is separated from the external world: the figure of host and guest, or observer and observed, which predominated in the description of sensation is repeated here within the realm of the "mind" itself.

The discussion of reflection, therefore, even while asserting the differences between this activity and that of sensation, extends and draws out the implications of the figuration that governed the description of sensation and the argument concerning it. The figure of movement from outside to inside, and the implicit personification of mind and sense, have become the personification of "powers" or "faculties" and a reflective "understanding." Just as motion permitted a visual portrayal of sensation as the relation between mind and sense, power permits a visualization of self-reflection as the relation between the mind and itself. The drama of sensation becomes the story of sensation, reflection, and a whole host of faculties.

This narrative, like the one in sensation, also tells a story of exposure and influence. Instead of exposure to an outside, the mind now finds itself exposed to itself in the form of its past. This becomes apparent in Locke's concern, in the *Essay* as elsewhere, with early childhood education. The movement between childhood, preserved through memory, and the present, like the movement between the sensory world and the mind, has a causal impact which appears in the narrative in the guise of influence:

> Children, when they come first into it, are surrounded with a world of new things, which, by a constant solicitation of their senses, draw the mind constantly to them . . . and so growing up in a constant attention to outward Sensations, seldom make any considerable Reflection on what passes within them, till they come to be of riper Years; and some scarce ever at all. (II.1.8)

The similarity of the roles of the sensory world and childhood in the discussion of sensation and reflection is particularly evident from the way they dovetail in this passage: childhood is the time when sensations are most influential. Indeed, the spatially conceived threat of sensation is placed here within the temporal framework of the concept of childhood, which is defined precisely as the *time* of sensory indulgence. This temporal category of the child contains a threat of its own analogous to that of sensation: that the past will perniciously influence the present, that it will prevent reflection from taking place. Childhood is indeed nothing other here than the name of the threatening relation between the mind and itself, conceived as a past and a present, a present mind threatened by a past one. Thus the child or childhood in this passage can no more simply be read literally than could motion in the earlier passages. Childhood is rather the figure of the understanding's distance from itself in its self-contemplation. Indeed, we could go so far as to say that the danger of sensation depends on its association *with* childhood, that is, that the figure of external imposition is a version of the fundamental figure of temporal imposition. Both are part of the story of self-disruption told by understanding when it looks upon itself. Attempting to observe itself, reflection tells a story of self-distance and self-division between past and present, and a continual reminder of this break is the helplessness of the mind before the violent intrusions of the sensory world.[26]

Both the spatial and temporal stories of origination thus tell of a break in the understanding's perception of itself. Moreover, since the child is a temporal category that necessitates a narrative account, it links this break in self-perception to the narrative form of the *Essay*. This pattern of displacement must affect how we understand Locke's "empiricism" and how we approach an interpretation of his text. Taken at face value, or for the doctrine it claims to give us, the *Essay* is first of all a philosophy of reflection which says that self-knowledge always takes the form of observation. In the *Essay*'s own reflections on the two sources of knowledge, however, the principles that govern the self-presentation of knowledge are closer to the conventions of literary writing than to the laws of visual perception. The very statement of the relation between visual perception and self-understanding is told as a story of power and influence: self-observation is mediated by self-narration. This disturbance of doctrine by story marks the intrusion of language into the self-contained territory of understanding, which had thought to establish itself in the transparency of self-contemplation. The functioning of formal literary features in the language of reflection, such as narrative and figure, creates a distance of interpretation between the understanding and itself, and between our understanding and this other understanding. It seems that this distance, this appearance of an unwanted third term, is a shadowy concern of the very plot of Locke's narrative, which tells of an understanding exposed to and often beleaguered by unwanted guests. Claiming its territory on the authority of the bodily eye, reason in Locke tells repeatedly of the excesses of this organ's power. This theme of sensory intrusion cannot be separated from the narrative form which intrudes on the self-transparency of the reason. The *Essay* is neither *simply* a doctrine nor *simply* a narrative, but a doctrine that tells itself only as narrative, or more accurately perhaps a narrative that dissimulates itself as doctrine.

If the *Essay* has something of "fiction" in it, however, this does not mean that it has nothing to teach. As with rumor, there is a "truth" at the heart of every fiction, and we can learn from Locke's narratives, if not exactly in the manner they intend. Indeed, the first thing we have learned from the discussions of sensation and reflection is that they cannot be judged on their own terms, or by their own criterion of truth and falsehood. This criterion involves, as we have seen, holding the "doctrine" up to "experience": accepting, first of all, a notion of "experience" as a testing ground and then deciding whether or not Locke's doctrine is adequate to it. This is an approach taken quite often not only in regard to Locke but in regard to philosophical texts in general: the philosophical demand to be judged as true or false and the empirical claim that the test of truth and falsehood is "experience" become the context in which many philosophical texts are read. But this sort of judging, far from achieving the evaluative distance it claims for itself, remains not only caught in the doctrine it reads, but also inscribed in its fiction. Locke's argument suggests that in order to learn from it we must take into account not only its doctrine, and not only its "formal" textual features, but the displacements occurring between them. This leaves us with several questions: What does the *particular* form of these displacements have to do with the particular claims of empirical doctrine? And if this text is neither *simply* truth nor *simply* fiction, what is it finally "about"?

These questions, imposed upon us by the first part of the *Essay,* are enough to indicate that empiricism extends far beyond what *others, as we noted in the introductory remarks, have often made of it. In Locke, at least, empiricism is neither simply a reductive doctrine of experience, nor even simply a doctrine at all, but a complex text that raises many questions about the interpretation of its own vocabulary. The second major claim concerning empiricism, however, is yet to be answered: the claim that empiricism provides no way of accounting for itself, or that it has no self-consciousness comparable to the critical and later speculative philosophies. It is here that the chapter on association demands consideration. It seems probable that this chapter has been so widely ignored because it *cannot* be understood in the context of this second claim concerning empiricism, that is, it can only be understood if it is seen as the outcome of the interpretive questions raised by the earlier parts of the *Essay*. It is, indeed, a chapter *about* fiction-making—the story-telling of the madman—and thus it introduces a topic that can hardly be treated in isolation from the issues raised in the other chapters. The relation between them, however, is not explicit, and it is the elaborate evasions of this chapter's self-criticism that make up the uniquely empirical character of its self-commentary and provide the greatest challenge to a non-empirical reading of the text.

Association

The chapter on the association of ideas, added in the fourth edition of the *Essay* in 1700, is an attempt to grapple with the one mental phenomenon to which reflection does not have immediate access, that is, the fact of madness, which Locke describes as a universal phenomenon that lies at the basis of all strong feelings of like and dislike. It might seem odd to find a chapter on madness in the middle of a work asserting the ultimate rationality of the mind; madness is precisely that one phenomenon which is neither like nor accessible to experience, and hence represents an otherness that would seem to pose great difficulties for a philosophy that asserts the full power of self-reflection over the entire realm of understanding. The attempt to bring madness *within* the realm of rational self-understanding, to incorporate what Locke describes as a self-blindness into the empirical system of self-observation, would suggest that the *Essay* may be attempting to deal with the emergence of a principle that exceeds rational understanding, a principle that seemed to operate, within the *Essay,* in its own narratives of entrapment. Indeed, as we shall see, the arguments of the madman do resemble very much the arguments of the *Essay* itself, and we can say that in attempting to incorporate madness into its rational self-enclosure, the *Essay* is also trying to account for and thus assimilate what resists understanding from within it.[27]

The first way in which the chapter confronts the earlier framework of the *Essay* is by introducing a sort of object of reflection which is not perceived by the usual reflective means:

> There is scarce any one that does not observe something that seems odd to him, and is in it self really Extravagant in the Opinions, Reasonings, and Actions of other Men. The least flaw of this kind, if at all different from his own, every one is quick-sighted enough to espie in another, and will by the Authority of Reason forwardly condemn, though he be guilty of much greater Unreasonableness in his own Tenets and conduct, which he never perceives, and will very hardly, if at all, be convinced of. (II.33.1)

Unlike the "ideas" treated in other chapters, the "flaw" in reasoning with which this chapter is concerned resists self-observation and is "espied" only in others. This phenomenon (or better non-phenomenon) which Locke later calls "madness" thus disrupts, to some extent, the certainty of self-knowledge and puts into question the sort of "perception" with which it is observed. The relation between this object and the perceiving mind is not direct but goes by way of a third party; the object "appears" only in the guise of another. In the first place, then, merely by virtue of this difference in the structure of the relationship of object and argument, the chapter immediately raises questions about the completeness of the concept of self-reflection on which the earlier parts of the book are modeled. This argument implicitly suggests that there is at least one type of self-reflection that does not take the simple form of reflective transparency, and involves a sort of interpretive self-distance. In so doing the chapter implies that its own form of argumentation, since it concerns what can only be seen in others, is not itself based on straightforward self-reflection. The confrontation with the indirection of madness produces a kind of argument which is itself unlike the usual form of rational reflection.

This sense of an implicit self-encounter between the empirical argument and its own narrative indirection emerges in the chapter in the similarity between the madness it describes and its own attempts to account for it empirically. While madness cannot be observed directly in oneself, the chapter claims nonetheless to treat it empirically, that is, to "trace this sort of Madness to the root it springs from, and so explain it, as to shew whence this flaw has its Original in very sober and rational Minds, and wherein it consists" (II.33.3). This encounter of empirical explanation and madness produces the following definition of the alien phenomenon:

> Some of our Ideas have a natural Correspondence and Connexion one with another: It is the Office and Excellency of our Reason to trace these, and hold them together in that Union and Correspondence which is founded in their peculiar Beings. Besides this there is another Connexion of *Ideas* wholly owing to Chance or Custom; *Ideas* that in themselves are not at all of kin, come to be so united in some Mens Minds, that 'tis very hard to separate them, they always keep in company, and the one no sooner at any time comes into the Understanding but its Associate appears with it; and if they are more than two which are thus united, the whole gang always inseparable shew themselves together. (II.33.5)

Once again, we encounter familiar company: the unwanted guests have shown up again, this time pictured as stranger-thoughts trying to pass themselves off as relatives at reason's family gatherings. Indeed, what was before merely a matter of the *origins* of thought in sensation and reflection is shown in madness to be a potential for all of the mind's reasoning activity: every rational connection of ideas threatens to be plagued by an importunate outsider who pushes his way in on thought and plants his obscene presence in the way of proper thinking; and this rapidly expands in the passage into a vision of the mad understanding as virtually stampeded by gangs of impostors, all of them, to use Wordsworth's expression, "claiming manifest kindred" with all of the others.[28] Madness would indeed seem to be an extension of the potential marked out in sensation and reflection.

The argument, as a definition and explanation, would attempt to control this madness by explaining it in terms of an empirical model that brings it back within the self-transparency of reflection.[29] The passage states not only the symptom of the illness, the uniting of ideas "that are not at all of kin," but attributes a cause as well, by suggesting that the connection of ideas is "owing to Chance or Custom." By placing the *cause* of association in an empirical event (a chance occurrence) or an empirical circumstance (custom), the argument reduces the mad activity, the binding of unrelated ideas, to the same order of experience as reasoning: what is different or other about association according to this passage is essentially what differs in the empirical circumstances in which the reasoning takes place, or with which the reasoning is concerned. Much as sensation and reflection are explained in terms of "external" and "internal" origins, association is explained in terms of the empirical context of the reasoning person. The argument contains the difference of mad association by displacing its *cause* onto its *circumstances* (or empirical origins), which are fully perceivable.

However, in its very attempt to maintain empirical integrity, the empirical explanation of madness comes to resemble the very madness it explains. In this passage there is a close connection between the experience of madness, which is itself a kind of interpretive activity, and the structure of the argument. The madman, we are told, suffers from the mistaking of a false connection of ideas for a true one; he misunderstands a false kinship between ideas for a true "correspondence" founded in their "peculiar beings." The argument likewise begins as a formal analysis of a distinction between true and false connections and of the cause of the latter, and rapidly slips into a narrative based on the substitution of empirical circumstances for conceptual causes. And much as "chance connections" come to have affective power for the madman, so the first connective in the passage, "Besides"—itself suggestive of the accident of contiguity—resolves itself into a story with its own persistent intrusiveness in the *Essay*. The madman's entrapment by his own fictions is in fact not unlike the argument's persistent return to the same story, the story of forced reception.[30]

This structural affinity between illness and argument deepens as the chapter continues. The "non-experience" that the chapter faces looks increasingly like a form of empirical argument. Toward the end of the chapter the illness is characterized as a sort of self-persuasive story-telling:

> Interest . . . cannot be thought to work whole Societies of Men to so universal a Perverseness, as that every one of them to a Man should knowingly maintain Falshood . . . there must be something that blinds their Understandings, and makes them not see the falshood of what they embrace for real Truth. That . . . will . . . be found to be what we are speaking of: some independent *Ideas*, of no alliance to one another, are by Education, Custom, and the constant din of their Party, so coupled in their Minds, that they always appear there together . . . This . . . is the foundation of the greatest, I had almost said, of all the Errors in the World . . . it hinders Men from seeing and examining. When two things in themselves disjoin'd, appear to the sight constantly united; if the Eye sees these things rivetted which are loose, where will you begin to rectify the mistakes that follow in two *Ideas*, that they have been accustom'd so to join in their Minds, as to substitute one for the other, and, as I am apt to think, often without perceiving it themselves? (II.33.18)

Here association is explicitly a matter of *self*-blindness: the emphasis of this passage, as of the other, is not so much on the falsity of the connections that are made as on the relation of reason to this falsity. The illness is not just the committing of error, but the unalterable experience of error as truth. For this reason the association is also called a "substitution," which refers less to the "unnatural connection" of ideas itself, than to the unawares replacement of the true connection with the false one. "Substitution" thus designates as much an affective state as a cognitive one: it is an act of self-persuasion, both the concocting of a fiction and the belief in it. The fiction is the bringing together of two accidentally related ideas, which are then given the title of "natural connection." Association thus inscribes the fiction of the connection into a narrative, in which the connection is given a "natural" origin. The fictional aspect of the narrative is the connection it attributes to the ideas; the persuasive aspect is the truth which it attributes to itself, in the name of the "natural origin." Implicit in associative reasoning is a sort of misguided self-reflection, that is, a self-interpretation. Whereas true reasoning would bask in the immediate reflection on its own certainty, association fails to see, yet continues to think, "blindly," by substitution—that is, it tells a story to itself.[31]

The chapter thus encounters in association a narrativizing not unlike its own, but recognized in the guise of the madness as "error." In this way, like the madness of which it tells, the empirical argument could be said to "recognize" its own strategies, but only in an other; it maintains the fiction of reflective truth by discovering interpretive error in "madness." Its own perspicuity, the striking insight of the argument into madness, is itself a symptom which, like the madman's symptoms, must be interpreted. The claim to reflective truth must be read, that is, as a symptom, or figure, of the fictionality of its claims. In the passage just quoted, this occurs by means of the argument's own "substitution." Having noted the universality, and by implication the apparent necessity of such self-blindness, the passage searches for "something that blinds their understandings." What it finds, however, is not a true cause, but "Education, Custom, and the constant din of their Party"—three similar cultural phenomena, the first of which Locke has explicitly shown, earlier, to be an effect and not a cause of association, and in any case would offer only a circumstance, rather than a cause for substituting. This permits the passage to continue with a reiteration of the artificial nature of associative connections—a concept that is fully within the realm of understanding—rather than with a fuller examination of the principle of the blindness itself—a nonexperience that resists empirical knowledge. As in the earlier explanation of association in terms of "Chance or Custom," here the description of the "unnatural" nature of the connection takes the place of an explanation of why the connection was made, and why it is so universally prevalent. The fact that the substituted term in the association is suggested by chance becomes itself an explanatory concept, namely that the substitution itself is accidental, that the law that governs it is chance itself. The argument's introduction of the term *substitution*, then, to describe the operations of the madman, is symptomatic, because while ostensibly describing the madman's mental act, it bespeaks the linguistic act of the argument. Associative "substitution" is the form in which the empirical argument confronts its own displacements.

We are presented, then, in this chapter, with a sort of empirical madness, or more familiarly, an empirical neurosis. We can understand the general principle of this neurosis in terms of the word *accident*, which occurs several times in this chapter as a synonym for *chance*, and is the definitive term in describing what is false about association. The "accidental Connexion of two ideas," and the "annexing" of "accidental ideas" to certain others,[32] generally refer to the circumstances that brought the ideas together: two ideas happened to appear in some event or situation together, and thus their connection was suggested "by chance" or "by accident." The accident is the empirical event that suggests the connection, one that is at some point made use of in a reasoning process. The "unnatural" nature of the connection, however, is a separate matter from the accidental nature of the circumstances that suggest it: the former holds regardless of how the connection was in fact suggested. In this sense, the connection is "accidental" not because it is suggested accidentally but because it is not "essential." Thus elsewhere Locke speaks of "accidents" as opposed to "essences."[33] This sense of accidental, as nonessential, and the sense of accidental as "having been suggested by accident" are juxtaposed in Locke's argument, or rather the shift from one to the other serves in lieu of an explanation: accidental (inessential) connections are made because of accidental empirical events. The pun on *accident* permits a shift from analysis to narrative, from the cause of making inessential connections to the story of the empirical circumstances that provided the material for the substitution. But this narrative, as certain as it is of its truth, returns repeatedly to the dangers of the experiential world it introduces. The emphasis on empirical accident as a controlling power reveals that it operates as a figure in a story. Much as we might say of persons that their obsession with external chance displaces a concern over an "inner" problem, so we can say that the "thematic" role of chance in the argument displaces its "formal" role as a figure.[34]

So far, then, the chapter has permitted some critical distance from its own method of argumentation by attempting to "explain" a sort of explanation that is very much like its own. As a result, the argument has itself introduced a nonempirical, indeed a rhetorical terminology by which it can itself be read: the notion of substitution (the notion of substituting ideas for one another, similar to the classical definition of the "trope" in rhetoric). By means of this concept we can identify the principle by which empiricism itself works as rhetorical, rather than visual. Empirical arguments, we learn, work by a sort of slippage from analytical distinctions to empirical narratives. This displaces pure self-reflection onto the contemplation of a "world," and the recognition of the role of language in the argument onto the belief in reflective clarity. Read as symptoms, these argumentative displacements seem to suggest that something is being "avoided." Like the madman, the empirical argument looks elsewhere and remains blind to itself, while yet permitting nonetheless a kind of oblique recognition to take place. These arguments, therefore, are not structured like perception, but like association, and it is the insistence on reflective certainty, or on experiential grounds, that is the first symptom of this "illness."

The narrative of madness and the narrative of empiricism encounter each other, most effectively, around the story of childhood origins, where the figures of the child and of sensation again come into play. One of the first examples of associative madness is the hypothetical case of the man who hates honey:

> A grown Person surfeiting with Honey, no sooner hears the Name of it, but his Phancy immediately carries Sickness and Qualms to his Stomach, and he cannot bear the very *Idea* of it; other *Ideas* of Dislike and Sickness, and Vomiting presently accompany it, and he is disturb'd, but he knows from whence to date this Weakness, and can tell how he got this Indisposition: Had this happen'd to him, by an over dose of Honey, when a Child, all the same Effects would have followed, but the Cause would have been mistaken, and the Antipathy counted Natural. (II.33.7)

The experience of disgust at the idea of honey is, according to the madman's associative reasoning, based on a "natural" connection of the ideas of honey and of sickness, a connection established presumably in the very creation of the individual. Empirical reasoning establishes that this connection is in fact based on a chance event in childhood, the overeating of honey, which brought together the ideas of sickness and honey. With the forgetting of the event, the natural connection of honey and sweetness is replaced by the connection of honey and sickness, because the empirical event connecting sickness and overeating has been forgotten. The mad honey-hater, however, grounds his experience of disgust in something external to his experience, that which is "natural" to him, so that the story of the real trauma is replaced by the story of the ideal event of his creation. The story's special power resides in its avoidance of trauma by making this trauma appear as the moment of creation.

The explanatory power of the argument, on the other hand, rests on a substitution of its own. This takes place when the argument claims to explain the *cause* of the madman's blind substitution by referring it to the passage from childhood to adulthood, or more specifically the natural forgetting that takes place in such a passage. That childhood should be forgotten does not, in fact, explain why this forgetting should take the form of a substitution of an accidental for a necessary connection, and we could take this one step further and say that the physiological change from childhood to adulthood does not explain the *mental* fact that childhood is forgotten. Thus, just as in the madman's associative self-misunderstanding, the accidental connection between honey and sickness replaces the empirical connection between overeating and sickness, so in the argument's reasoning the empirical change from childhood to adulthood substitutes for a genuine cause of the forgetting or of its abnormal form as substitution. That is, the physiological loss of childhood is used to "explain" the mental forgetting of childhood experience; and the empirical basis of the former "history" gives to the latter "explanation" the appearance of descriptive truth. Similarly, the "cause" of the madness becomes displaced onto the empirical origin in the childhood event of overeating, and the explanation turns into a narrative. In this story, the child, as a set of experiences that are forgotten, becomes a figure of self-blindness; the danger of childhood, of which we were warned in the discussion of reflection, is shown to be a figure for the dangers of self-blindness or "substitution." If the madman's story of creation avoids the traumas of his childhood, the argument's story of childhood avoids its own rhetorical trauma. Madman and empiricist are inextricably linked, that is, in the narration of their ignorance of a trauma.

The event of overeating also operates around a figure, one which we have already seen closely connected with childhood, that of sensation. Just as the forgetting of childhood is said to be natural, so is the surfeiting ascribed to natural causes. But we can, of course, ask why the child eats too much honey. Is it an accident? Or is it that "solicitation of the senses" spoken of earlier? We are told, here, not just the story of an "antipathy," but of a "sympathy" in excess—of desire exceeding physical capacities.[35] Sensation, like childhood, is a figure for an event that is not itself empirically observable. The configuration of the two in the story of the honey is thus not simply based on empirical fact; it is a configuration which borrows empirical fact in order to make possible a certain kind of narrative, which avoids a certain kind of trauma.

This "borrowing" of the empirical world can be called the "aesthetic" dimension of the empirical argument. Empirical facts—like physiological childhood and the mechanics of sensation—as they are inscribed in a narrative, give the illusion of description, or that the argument is talking about "the world" or "experience." The linguistic form of the argument thus disappears behind the fiction of pure self-reflection: self-knowledge appears to itself in the form of empirical light rather than in the form of language. This is an "aesthetic" pattern both in the popular sense of a fictional representation presenting oneself to oneself safely, i.e. without full recognition, and in the stricter sense of bringing light to that which is not by nature visual, in this case language. This function is, itself, governed by rhetorical principles; it is a form of persuasion, the imposing of the fiction that the argument is talking only about the empirical world.

The separation between observed "illness" and observing "argument" is a part of this fiction, for the relation between the object of the argument and the argument itself is in fact governed by figurative rather than perceptual laws. This figure is structured around the notions of accident and necessity, which we mentioned above. The madman, having made an "accidental" connection, calls it necessary: in the example, the adult says he naturally hates honey; the argument, having uncovered a certain necessity, the manifestation of a universal self-blindness, calls it accidental: in the example, the text ascribes the self-deception to a chance event in childhood and its chance forgetting. Thus, while association substitutes the name "necessary" for that of "accidental," the empirical argument substitutes the name "accident" for "necessity." The relationship between illness and argument is thus governed by the figure of chiasmus. In this figure, the apparent opposition of the two sides is subordinated to a larger symmetry, which reveals a close affinity between them.[36] The fact that the madman appears to be an innatist, a doctrine that Locke explicitly opposes, does not in fact change the similarity of their structure: just as the madman claims a natural ideal cause of his antipathy, which is beyond his control, so the *Essay* (both in this chapter and elsewhere) claims an empirical ground, a "source," for its knowledge. Both origins are considered "external" to the creation of the argument itself, and both are considered "natural." The symptom of this hidden affinity is the similarity in the consequences of each argument: if the madman becomes prey to "nature," something over which he claims he has no control, Locke's argument leads to a fatalism of chance, in which any empirical event can "cause" a disruption of proper reasoning. Both the madman, or neurotic, and empirical reasoning claim merely to "observe" what they have in fact "made." The figurative nature of this similarity reveals its rhetorical effects, of addressing the problems of empirical argumentation in the guise of experience, of confronting the fictions that empiricism has written as if they were seen.[37]

If we step back for a moment and place this chapter in the context of the earlier sections on sensation and reflection, we can understand better its self-critical function. This chapter is not critical in the strict sense, as questioning, thematically, the conditions of possibility of understanding; however, it can be considered to have critical characteristics in so far as the structure of its argument foregrounds the features of the argument *as* argument, or the means by which the understanding it achieves is made possible by textual strategies. The similarities between madman and empirical argument within the chapter indicate that the structure of the empirical argument, its "formal" features, can be understood as versions of "associative reasoning" or rhetorical fiction-making. This, of course, we began to be aware of in our own reading of the first sections. But when the *Essay* itself reveals this fact, it also tells us that the rhetorical effect of this fiction-making is the displacement of self-reflection onto the observation of another. This means specifically, for the empirical argument, that its claim to be a transparent self-reflection of "understanding" is a figurative displacement of the actual way in which understanding, in the argument, comes to know itself: that is, as a narrative. In this way the figurative patterns of the text—such as the relation between madness and argument—function rhetorically; they seem to record a perceptual relationship rather than a figurative one. Empirical argumentation can thus further be understood as an aesthetic: the names of empirical objects and acts are borrowed for the purpose of bringing light to the argument's language. It is not common to think of empiricism as an aesthetic; this term is generally reserved for critical and post-critical arguments. But Locke's empiricism shares, with these other aesthetics, the attempt to mediate self-understanding by means of "experience," even if this experience is not said specifically to involve art; and this mediation has the same effect of subordinating the language of the philosophical text to the "appearance" of the "idea." Empiricism involves a different strategy but not an entirely different set of issues as aesthetic philosophies. The chapter on association thus demands, along with a reconsideration of how its texts are read, a reconsideration of its positioning among philosophical "traditions."

The power of this aesthetic strategy, or the mode of self-reflection that appears in the association chapter, can be gauged by the effectiveness of its explanations. To say that experience is a type of figuration permits one to say that figuration is a type of experience, and it is by this logic that the association chapter develops. It is this self-reflective power that would seem to have made the examples so effective as demystifications of a certain self-mythologizing represented by madness. That is, the effectiveness of these explanations lies less in their empirical truth than in their negative power to provide a critique of the self-mythologizing of *other* forms of narrative. And it is this function that appears to have given these examples in Locke's chapter the venerable status of "the first case histories," a form of explaining madness that has come down to us most prominently in the narrative explanations provided by psychoanalysis.

Madness, then, in the association chapter, is an aestheticization of empirical argumentation, a way of understanding its linguistic strategies in non-linguistic terms. And within such a framework of understanding—that is, in the story of the madman—we are told that the "reason" for the displacements of empirical arguments is the avoidance of a trauma at the "origins." But we have not been told *what* that trauma is; while we know that the empirical argument is a narrative and that its fictions are figurative displacements, we do not know exactly what they displace. The vocabulary of substitution, which mediates between mental and linguistic behaviour, still conceals a traumatic "origin" that the chapter has so far managed to contain within its own fictions. If, as part of this fiction, empirical accident becomes a figure for linguistic necessity, what, we might ask, *is* this necessity? What "trauma" conceals itself within the displacements of the argument?

Mourning and Melancholia

Reading further into the chapter, we encounter an example of an illness that seems to foreground the argument's associative fictions. This is the case of a mother endlessly mourning her dead child, a mother who, unlike the healthy mourner, does not give up her grieving after a reasonable interval, and continues to sorrow until her death (an anticipation of Freud's distinction between mourning and melancholia).[38] This child-adult relationship appears to have a special significance in Locke; it is one of the two examples that reappear in the *Conduct of the Understanding,* and it also appears, somewhat altered, in an earlier part of the *Essay,* "Of Retention" (II.10.5). In addition, the portrayal of the child-adult relationship in this example seems to provide a sort of commentary on this relationship as it figures in the earlier examples; indeed, it seems to bear a similar relation to these as these bear to the figure of the child in the rest of the *Essay.* In each case the negative relation between child and adult becomes more radical; in the earlier example of association, the relationship of child and adult is determined by blindness, while in this example their relationship is determined by death. As we have seen, the significance of the figure of childhood has been to dramatize the argument's own strategies, to serve as a figure for an original "trauma" as well as for the forgetting or displacing of this trauma. We might consider the dead child, then, as a second-order figure, as a figure of the figure of self-blindness. In this context, the example appears to offer a way of approaching the issues raised by the earlier examples, that is, what is the textual "trauma" that is displaced in the neurosis of empiricism.

The peculiarity of this illness is first of all evident in its description not as a forgetting but as a remembering:

> *Ideas* in our Minds, when they are there, will operate according to their Natures and Circumstances; and here we see the cause why Time cures certain Affections, which Reason, though in the right, and allow'd to be so, has not power over, nor is able against them to prevail with those who are apt to hearken to it in other cases. The Death of a Child, that was the daily delight of his Mother's Eyes, and joy of her Soul, rends from her Heart the whole comfort of her Life, and gives her all the torment imaginable; use the Consolations of Reason in this case, and

> you were as good preach Ease to one on the Rack, and hope to allay, by rational Discourses, the Pain of his Joints tearing asunder. Till time has by disuse separated the sense of that Enjoyment and its loss from the *Idea* of the Child returning to her Memory, all Representations, though never so reasonable, are in vain; and therefore some in whom the union between these *Ideas* is never dissolved, spend their Lives in Mourning, and carry an incurable Sorrow to their Graves. (II.33.13)

The introduction of death into the events in the narrative completely changes the nature of the "blindness" represented by this illness. "Time" now becomes, not the agent of illness, but the agent of its cure, a cure which is not to remember properly but rather to forget. This reversal in the function of time is closely connected with a curious emphasis on causality: causal connection is emphasized both earlier in the passage ("and here we see the cause") and later ("and therefore") without the slightest attempt to provide adequate grounds for the assertion. When time, that is, becomes the cure rather than the cause of the illness—when the cure is not remembering but forgetting—the causal logic behind the previous empirical explanations of association becomes inadequate. If we think of this example as a sort of commentary on the "trauma" behind empirical figurations, this shift indicates that it cannot be conceived in the same terms; it does not permit translation, as do the terms *blindness* and *substitution,* into the narratives of childhood events and forgetting. If the example of the mourning mother's behavior tells us something about the "trauma" behind empirical displacements, it is first of all that this "event" is not itself a type of substitution.

The nature of this nonsubstitutive association becomes more evident in the attempt of the argument to make it fit the normal associative pattern. Through the curative function of time, Locke says, the mother would be able to forget the death of the child or to "separate" the idea of the child's loss from the idea of the child—a separation that takes place in healthy mourning. Locke thus implies that the endlessly mourning mother unnaturally connects "the sense of that Enjoyment [of the child] and its loss" with "the Idea of the Child": in other words, whenever the mother remembers the child that has died, she remembers its death; she substitutes death for the life of the child and thus confuses an unnatural connection for what is naturally connected with the child. The unwanted company, the idea that keeps "returning" with the idea of the child and claiming kinship, is that of death. But this is an unsettling use of associative explanation. For death is not an empirical property among others: it is not part of a fully known "experience" that could be shared by mother and child and, hence, could become part of a system of "natural" and "unnatural" relations. In the child's death, rather, the mother faces only an absence, a blank. And this absence, moreover, is precisely what is proper to the child: in dying, the child is properly connected with the idea of death. Indeed, "death" becomes the child's *only* "property" because in dying it loses all empirical properties whatsoever, and the term *dead* now names precisely this absenting of the child from the world of perceptual qualities. The mother's remembering of the death cannot be a matter of accidents and essences, therefore, because what is "proper" to the child is, now, precisely that it has no properties: in dying the child does not "have an accident," but becomes an accident of the event that now subsumes its whole being. The mother's error would seem to consist not in a substitution of one perceptual property for another, not in a substitution of ideas, but in the insistent linking of the idea of the child with what is not a perception at all.

Considered in terms of the other examples, mourning represents a shift out of the system of "true" and "false" connections; it marks instead the difference between the system "connections-associations" and another way of establishing meaning. If we read this new illness, as we have suggested, not as *another* illness but as a condition or moment of "regular" madness, then mourning tells us two things about association. First, taken out of its context in the argument and considered only as a mental illness, the mother-child example suggests that the self-forgettings of association are ultimately versions of mourning, the fictions of a self that experiences itself as an absence, and attempts to fill this in with something it can recognize. The "true" connection which lies at the heart of associations is not a trauma to the self but the lack of a self. Thus the traumas of experience which association avoids can finally be reduced to this single trauma, this original self-absence; associative substitutions are displaced versions of the attempt to establish a unified self-consciousness. Placed in context, as part of the argument and not as a fact in itself, this "melancholic" basis of substitution points to a lack within the argument that its own figurative borrowings of empirical fact constantly fill up. The "mourning" at the basis of the argument's "neurosis" is not a substitution of one term for another but a sort of linguistic trauma of self-absence.

What is it, then, that is "wrong" with the mourning mother? What constitutes her mad excess? We have seen that her illness cannot be judged in terms of substitutions or true and false connections. The problem with the mother's "remembering," indeed, is that it is not a remembering at all, any more than it is a forgetting. Its only excess or abnormality is in its attempt to establish a relationship which is something *like* that of remembering, with an object that has lost its empirical status—or rather with no object at all. The impropriety of the endlessly mourning mother is precisely that she attempts to remember the child properly, as it properly is—that is, in its death; the thought of "its loss" always "accompanies" her memory. Unlike the unwelcome "company" of association by substitution, this idea is improper not because it is false but because it is not a true property at all. By remembering death as the property of her child, the mother gives her child to death as *its* property; she gives it a form, a means of appearing. The mother, wishing to fight death with her memory, unknowingly adorns death with the face of her child. What is "wrong" with the mother, as the argument presents it, is that she cannot remember her child without turning the child into the figure of death.[39]

The real danger of the mother's behavior, then, is not falsehood, but the reversal by which thought turns its objects into figures. But the figure in the mother's remembering is not the "associative" figuration based on the substitution of one idea or term for another by means of an analogy grounded in perception. Since the child is no longer strictly speaking a perceptual presence, the remembering of it is not a substitution of terms, or a trope, but a prosopopoeia, the lending of figure to an absence, giving face to the dead.[40] The mother's act, the attempt to establish a thought in the absence of a real object, is thus irreducible either to perception or to thought; unlike substitution, prosopopoeia cannot be given either sensory equivalents or psychical equivalents such as repression or defense. The "trauma" this figure creates for understanding would lie in the nature of the reversal which the figure effects in thought: by establishing itself by means of an imposed figuration, the self can only recognize itself *as figure*—not a figure that could lead back to a perception, but one that is no longer part of any conceivable experience. This threat would seem to be represented, in the passage on mourning, by the death which inhabits the figure of the child. For this threatens to turn all narratives of childhood into allegories of death: to turn the self, through its self-remembering, into the story of its own death.

We can fully grasp the import of this threat, however, only by seeing how it enters into the empirical argument that attempts to encounter and control, or explain away this "madness." The passage says, as we have seen, that the illness lies in the connection the mother makes between death and the child. The cure can only come about, we read, when "time has by disuse separated the sense of that Enjoyment and its loss from the idea of the Child returning to her Memory," that is, when the idea of the child is (properly) connected only with its past life, rather than with its present death. But in thus attempting to explain the mother's figuring act as error, the argument produces an even more far-reaching deformation of its own. We can think of this in two ways. First, most simply, that in this passage, to remember the child properly means, necessarily, to remember it improperly, that is, as separate from the state it is in fact in. More specifically, to separate the idea of the dead child from its death is equally to separate the idea of the living child from its life; if the dead child is to be remembered properly apart from the property of death, then the properties of death and life are no longer proper or essential to the idea of the child in general. At this point, the word *child*, which has been the centering figure of meaning in this passage, the place in which the distinction between madness and sanity takes place, comes to mean something neither dead nor alive; it becomes half-dead and half-alive, a kind of zombie. In saving the child from death, from the deformations of prosopopoeia, the argument does not give it life, but rather something like a suspension between life and death, something perhaps more fearful even than the figure the mother produces.

The empirical argument, then, itself works through a kind of distorting, nonsubstitutive figuration. For the word *child* can thus no longer be read literally as the name of an empirical object, nor can it be read figuratively as substituting for the concept of self-blindness. The word *child* is, indeed, not literal here, although its figuration is not a substitution, but rather a naming of something without a name, the imposition of figure on the nameless which creates a sort of "abusive" or monstrous entity. This imposed figure is called, in rhetorical handbooks, "catachresis," and is defined as a kind of "abuse" of figure.[41] It is traumatic to the argument because of a reversal like that in prosopopoeia: in the very establishing of a ground of certainty—empirical experience—the language of empiricism deprives itself of any fully comprehensible experiential status. The manner in which the *knowledge* of experience is achieved—the empirical argument—is the means by which one permanently loses the *certainty* of experience; every time the argument *claims* as *understanding* to know itself, via experience, it *tells* of its disruption of this self-knowledge as *text*. And this text is not, indeed, within experiential grasp: the half-dead child that is given in this example is no child one would ever encounter in the empirical world.

The central figure of empirical self-understanding, then, the face of the child, is the very place in which empiricism loses the transparency of self-observation, and comes up against itself as a monstrous unnameable. With this loss in self-transparency, the self-enclosure of understanding is laid open in the very act that makes systematic self-understanding possible in the first place. The figure of the child's face—the figuration by which the *Essay* gives face or form to understanding, by which understanding knows itself—is also a disfiguration of this self-knowledge, a defacement of the empiricist. In the passage, this disfiguring activity seems to be shadowed in the use of a figure of physical disarticulation, the representation of the mother's experience of remembering as the pain of her joints "tearing asunder" on the rack. The threat of endless mourning, of the madness of melancholia, appears to be a kind of disarticulation of empirical language itself, a tearing asunder of the system by the figure that first established its articulated motion. And, indeed, it is not only the mad mother, but also the cure, or the understanding of the empiricist, which tears asunder: health can only be achieved, Locke says, when "time has by disuse *separated* the sense of that Enjoyment and its loss from the *Idea* of the Child."

The relation between the prosopopoeia of the mother and the catachresis of the argument thus differs from the chiastic relation between association and figuration. This chiasmus, as we interpreted it, represented a negative self-reflection of the argument, made possible by the mediating term *substitution*. The argument staged itself, there, as neurosis. Here, the mother does not do something *like* that of the argument; she does not "represent" empirical reasoning; rather she is the only form in which the sort of giving-of-figure called catachresis can be read. Prosopopoeia in the example is the act of an *agent*, a mother; it is a giving of a *face* that is modeled, presumably, on the face of the one who is giving it. The argument's catachresis, on the other hand, names an act that makes all faces and agents possible; it is the condition of possibility of face-giving. But this act is no sooner named than it is read as the act *of someone*, as a figure within a system of figures that has been created and named by an agent which has a face and a hand to write. The shift beween catachresis and prosopopoeia is the moment when language is itself inscribed in an empirical argument, in which it is "part of" experience—either written or spoken. And once language is read empirically, the whole world comes with it: sensation, reflection, and the world they encounter. The world becomes humanly experienced, and there is nothing that isn't *part of* our experience. This "part of" marks the power of empirical reasoning, which can contain any text within the experiential framework, but it also tells more obliquely of the parting-of-ways which marks the establishment of empirical knowledge in the empirical world, the turning of the empirical world into a pretext for the text of empiricism.

We can finally approach an answer to our question of what empirical arguments are "about"—over and beyond what they claim as their subject—if they are read as narratives and not as doctrines. The obsession with causes and origins in empirical narratives can be read, now, not as mere reductiveness, an ignoring of the rich activity of mental life, but as a (not-)telling of the conditions of empirical language. The stories of influence, of the dangers of the origin—of the sensory origin in the external world, or the reflective origin in childhood—tell, also, of the excesses of the language which made possible the claims of the empirical argument. Far from being able to take the language of empirical experience at face value—to "see" what Locke "means"—we must reread the dangerous "externality" of experience in terms of the disruption, not "within" meaning but "of" meaning as it is established through the imposition of sense. Thus the terminology of motion, which Locke specifies as being undefinable and hence known only by direct reference to experience, turns back on itself, and refers as much to linguistic as to sensory displacement; in fact the story of sensory "conveyance" can be read as the tale of the very means by which the naming of the sensory world in the empirical argument names the act of naming as well. The empirical deprivations of this "original" imposition are retold as the continuous influx of threatening "sensations" and the numerous self-deceptions of the divided understanding. Words such as *convey, perceive, organ,* and *nerve* each "refer" to a figurative drama unconnected with the empirical laws of nature. In Locke, it turns out, the most reductive empirical language is the most highly figurative language of all.[42]

Empirical arguments, then, not only *do* involve an attempt to "account for" themselves, but this is in fact practically all that they do, over and over again. In this sense the "melancholia" of endless mourning was an appropriate figure for the argument, since its repetitive return to the same story, the same event, is similar to the way in which the varied stories of empiricism tell the same story over and over again. The variety of the neurotic is seductive, and the empirical framework makes possible a seeming infinity of "personal" interpretations; but the free associations of the best empirical arguments merely distract from a deeper melancholic monotony. One might object that there is a great deal of empirical "truth" in, for example, the description of mental illness—that it is a surprisingly acute precursor to our own psychoanalytic case histories. But we might consider the possibility that this is not so much evidence of the power of reasoning based on the empirical observation of experience, but of the way in which our "experience" takes the form of empirical narratives. As psychoanalysts, and psychoanalyzed, we are empiricists; as empiricists, we are constantly telling the story of the nonempirical grounds of our own experience.

Conclusion

We have discovered that Locke's empiricism takes the form of a narrative, a narrative that tells a very specific tale about itself. We might now extend this somewhat and say that narratives, to the extent that they are readable, take the form of empirical arguments. This would seem to put us back in the same position as the critics against whom we originally defined our project. But empirical arguments, as we understand them, have very little in common with their experiential descriptions; it is precisely by means of the vocabulary of experience, I suggest, that the narratives of Romantic literature question their own referential status. One Romantic narrative that deserves an immediate reinterpretation in this context is that of the "associationist tradition": the fiction of a single derivation of eighteenth-century associationism from Locke is as elaborate a (Lockean) associationist fiction as any Romantic story. Such a rereading would certainly change the way in which we conceive of the genres and periods of empiricism and Romanticism—one might imagine a shift, for example, to a more text-oriented terminology for generic distinctions, or a new story of the Romantic period returning us to a "truer" associationism.[43] But at the least, such a change would bring to awareness our own textual yearnings toward the empirical world.

More immediately, perhaps, we can think of how a new empiricism will help us approach individual Romantic texts. In Wordsworth, for example, we may pay more attention to the vocabulary of experience which forms the context of the doctrine of imaginative growth. Who can say, for example, what words such as *child* and *mother, eye* and *mind* refer to in those seeming descriptions of the poet's empirical infancy? What reference will we give to words such as *eye* and *face,* and what "events" will we say the *Prelude*'s narrative relates? Wordsworth's vocabulary and narrative power have a powerful empirical appeal; but if we have learned anything from reading Locke, it is that it is precisely this empiricism which tells us not to take poets such as Wordsworth at "face value."

2

PAST RECOGNITION

Narrative Origins in Wordsworth and Freud

The word *ego* has a place in the discourse of Romantic literature, but to speak today of the "Romantic ego," or to read Romantic texts in terms of other psychoanalytic concepts, is necessarily to juxtapose two different discourses: Romantic and psychoanalytic.[1] And this is also to suggest that our self-understanding, as articulated within psychoanalytic discourse, can be understood historically, in terms of the relation between psychoanalytic theory and the texts of an earlier period called Romanticism. The nature of this gesture—the representation of self-knowledge as a history of its evolving discourses—is not entirely clear, but it is nevertheless entirely appropriate, since it is precisely this configuration of self-knowledge, history, and discourse which many "Romantic" texts explore. By reading these texts in a search for our past, therefore, we can learn more about this very attempt to recognize ourselves in them.

A similar gesture, although apparently inadvertent, is made by Jeffrey Mehlman in translating a passage from Freud's *Three Essays on Sexuality*. In the section explaining the sexual drive in terms of its origins in the nursing baby, Mehlman offers a new translation for the word *Anlehnung*, which designates the relation of the sexual drive to the instinct of hunger. In place of Strachey's "anaclisis," Mehlman suggests the word *propping*.[2]

The oddness of the word in this context recalls a striking use of it in Wordsworth's *Prelude:* after describing the origin of the poetic spirit in the baby at the breast, the poet refers to the mother as the "prop" of the child's affections. Mehlman's translation calls our attention to a problem common to the narratives of personal history in both texts. Each explains the dynamics of a self which cannot be called empirical (the sexual drive or poetic spirit) [3] in terms of its origins in an empirically situated event, the physical relation of the mother and the nursing baby. But this produces, in each text, two different stories, one of which describes an intimate affective relation between the baby and the mother's body, and another which is less concerned with affect, and less clearly a matter of subject and object, and which refers instead to a propping or leaning activity. The possibility of understanding Freud's and Wordsworth's narratives of self-knowledge revolves around the problem of reading these two stories together.

The importance of emphasizing the role of discourse in this problem, as we have done by focusing on the word *ego* and on Mehlman's translation, is suggested by both Wordsworth's and Freud's texts. The Blessed Babe passage in *The Prelude* locates the origins of "our first poetic spirit" in a "being" whose history moves from "mute dialogues with my mother's heart" to "conjectures" that "trace" this progress. [4] A "poetic spirit" is a "being" whose history is the mediation of two discourses, or who defines the difference between two discourses as its own history. The place of the empirical world in this history, and the distinction between the affective and propping stories in regard to it, bypass from the beginning any simple oppositions between language, self-knowledge, and the body, and concern rather differences in the configuration of these terms.

A similar framework is established in Freud's *Three Essays,* in which the patient's self-understanding is not strictly distinguishable from the language of the psychoanalytic interpretation. In describing the way psychoanalysis explains neurotic symptoms to certain patients, Freud says:

> With the help of their symptoms and other manifestations of
> their illness, [psychoanalysis] traces their unconscious thoughts
> and translates [*übersetzt*] them into conscious ones. In cases in
> which someone who has previously been healthy falls ill after an
> unhappy experience in love it is also possible to show with cer-
> tainty that the mechanism of his illness consists in a turning-
> back of his libido onto those whom he preferred in his infancy.[5]

The word *translates* identifies the process of becoming conscious with the linguistic "return" from a foreign language, the
"symptoms and other expressions" of the illness, to the mother
tongue. These symptoms turn away from, or translate figuratively, the unconscious thoughts, which are thus conceived of
as a "literal" meaning distorted by neurosis. When the literal
meaning is retrieved, however, it has become part of a history;
the unconscious thoughts are always ultimately revealed to be
infantile libidinal desires. The self recognizes itself, therefore,
as a relation between unconscious and conscious thoughts, and
narrates this relation as the history of the sexual drive. The
movement described by this narrative, between the sexual drive
and the narrative's own language of self-understanding, is made
possible by repression, which makes the drive appear as symptoms that can be read like a language.

The formation of symptoms also governs normal development in Freud's "affective" version of sexual origins. The development of sexuality in general involves the same negative activity of repression that operates in neurosis:

> At a time at which the first beginnings of sexual satisfaction are
> still linked with the taking of nourishment, the sexual instinct
> has a sexual object outside the infant's body in the shape of his
> mother's breast. It is only later that the instinct loses that object,
> just at the time, perhaps, when the child is able to form a total
> idea of the person to whom the organ that is giving satisfaction
> belongs. As a rule the sexual drive then becomes auto-erotic,
> and not until the period of latency has been passed through is
> the original relation restored. There are thus good reasons why
> a child sucking at his mother's breast has become the prototype

of every relation of love. The finding of an object is in fact a refinding of it.[6]

This narrative is structured very much like the interpretation of a neurosis: adult sexual relations are translated, like symptoms, into a history. The "refinding" of the object in "every relation of love" is in fact a displacement of the "original relation," a substitution which functions figuratively much like a neurotic symptom. Similarly, while the loss of the mother's breast is not described as a repression, it is nonetheless suggestive of it, as if the connection of the breast with the mother made the breast taboo, and the substitution of other objects necessary. Repression, then, results in adult sexual objects' serving as figurative substitutes for the mother's breast. This means, first of all, that repression makes all (adult) sexual relations symptomatic, and thus capable of being read and interpreted in a psychoanalytic narrative, which itself constitutes a moment of sexual development. It is repression which aligns the sexual drive with language; repression and psychoanalytic translation hold similar positions with regard to the drive, differentiated as before (symptoms) and after. Secondly, repression distorts a relation to a *physical* object; the breast is the empirical element that locates the origin of the drive. The figurative meaning of adult sexual objects depends on their substitution for the mother's real breast as their "literal" meaning.

The other story that Freud tells about the origins of the drive offers an alternative to this model of sexuality as repression and substitution. It is uncertain if any negativity, corresponding to repression, is operative here: "To begin with, sexual activity attaches itself to [props itself upon] functions serving the purpose of self-preservation and does not become independent of them until later . . . At its origin . . . it has as yet no sexual object."[7] Harold Bloom, following Laplanche, notes an important difference in this story from the first: there is no original sexual object in the breast itself; the only real object is the breast as a source of milk.[8] We could put this another way: the empirical relation of baby and breast—instinct and physical object—is replaced by the relation of drive and instinct, a displacement that is not a substitution, but a "propping." It is propping that makes the breast sexual, but only in fantasy; if, in Bloom's words, the first relation is "literal," sexuality is from the beginning figurative. The confusion of literal and figurative in the two stories, and the shifting status of repression, suggest that the principle that relates mind, body, and language may be difficult to determine.

We can further explore such configurations in Wordsworth in terms of the imaginative activity of poetry. The emphasis on imaginative transformation in *The Prelude* is part of a critical response to Hartleyan associationist psychology, a tradition out of which Freud's psychoanalytic theory, through the work of James Mill, also developed.[9] Freud's critique, centered on the concepts of drive and defense, is anticipated in the Wordsworthian dynamic of passion and memory. In Book Four of *The Prelude*, this dynamic operates through the figure of self-knowledge as a "reflection" which is also a motion:

> As one who hangs down-bending from the side
> Of a slow-moving boat upon the breast
> Of a still water, solacing himself
> With such discoveries as his eye can make
> Beneath him in the bottom of the deeps,
> . . . now is crossed by gleam
> Of his own image, by a sunbeam now,
> And motions that are sent he knows not whence,
> Impediments that make his task more sweet;
> Such pleasant office have we long pursued
> Incumbent o'er the surface of past time.
>
> (1805, 247–63)

Motion, here, is a figure of the continuity between past and present, a continuity upon which the similarity of physical reflection and memory depends. As the operation of a specifically poetic memory, furthermore, it is also the figure of figurative language, conceived of as the motion from one meaning to another. The words *hang, deeps,* and *gleam,* however—often associated in Wordsworth with imaginative figuration—suggest

that these motions are not necessarily straightforward, and, indeed, we can read this as a critique of the Hartleyan kinetics in
which natural motions caused and were continuous with cognitive and affective ones.[10] By reversing the direction of motion
and making it originate in the observer, the passage replaces
this simple kinetics with a more complex causality. The distorting function of the motion is thereby emphasized as the possibility of an affective gain, the "solacing" and "sweetness" of
what otherwise might be a less rewarding "task." Motion thus
also connotes its eighteenth-century meaning of "movement"
as e-motion, and the rhetoric of figurative substitution attains a
persuasive dimension. In this scene, then, memory is a form of
rhetorical self-persuasion, which could be said to reinterpret
associationist doctrine (as it was developed after Locke by philosophers such as Hume and Hartley) in terms of the rhetorical
tradition out of which it sprang.[11]

    This complex, distorting act is not in the least inimical to
self-knowledge, however, and indeed makes it possible. By
means of this rhetorical activity, the mere "eye" that looks into
the water receives a whole "image," or face in return: the motion from past to present is also a passage from eye to face, or a
totalization of the self by means of metonymical substitution.
The simultaneously distorting and supporting capacities of this
substitution are exemplified in the naming of the surface upon
which the boat moves as a "breast," the supportiveness of which
is both physical and affective. This also links the "solace" of the
memory to a very specific origin, which is both the empirical
relation of baby and breast, and the moment in the poem in
which the words "*breast*" and "*eye*" have a presumably "literal"
status. This is the Blessed Babe scene in Book Two, quoted
here in part:

> blest the babe
> Nursed in his mother's arms, the babe who sleeps
> Upon his mother's breast, who, when his soul
> Claims manifest kindred with an earthly soul,
> Doth gather passion from his mother's eye.
>
> (1805, 239–43)

This scene is also governed by the figure of passage, present here in the word *passion* as a sort of originary movement; and here, too, the breast supports an eye-to-face relationship. Indeed, the phrase in Book Four "crossed by his own image" describes the figurative structure of the two passages: the self-recognition of the poet is structured as a chiasmus, or crossing between past and present relations. If the relation of the poetic self to its past self, the babe, is like the relation of the babe to the mother, the continuity of the two is a crossing in which the babe becomes an object for itself (in poetic memory) and the eye of the mother is replaced by the figurative "eye" of the poetic self (the movement to self-consciousness).[12] The displacement of the eye thus governs a dialectical movement which mediates between self-consciousness and figurative language, by making the discursive figure akin to a phenomenal "image."

This cognitive-affective gain is achieved, however, at the price of a negation: the breast supports the transition between passion and memory only in its absence. Shortly after the Blessed Babe passage, the movement of substitutions begins again with the mother's death:

> For now a trouble came into my mind
> From unknown causes: I was left alone
> Seeking the visible world, nor knowing why.
> The props of my affections were removed,
> And yet the building stood, as if sustained
> By its own spirit. All that I beheld
> Was dear to me, and from this cause it came
> That now to Nature's finer influxes
> My mind lay open—to that more exact
> And intimate communion which our hearts
> Maintain with the minuter properties
> Of objects which already are beloved.
>
> (1805, 291–302)

The use of the word *influxes*—designating a moving inward— suggests that this passage too engages an associationist doctrine of motion. The critique of this doctrine involves an emphasis on the necessity of a destructive moment in order for motion to begin: the movement that leaves the mind open is first the "re-*moval*" of an impediment (the mother). Substitution occurs as a transformation of this negation into a positive gain: the "props" of the mother are replaced by the "properties" of nature in an act of "communion," the Christian connotations of which suggest the turning of death into life, and the dead letter into the living poetic figure. The association of this transformation with causality—the disturbing "unknown causes" which become a more positive "this cause"—also complicates the Hartleyan kinetics with the suggestion of a dynamic element, named earlier as the "gravitation and the filial bond" (1.263) of child and nature.

The phrase "unknown causes," however, and the reference to a "trouble," are somewhat obscure. It would seem that these causes are something other than the mother's death, since that is, presumably, known (and singular).[13] Yet perhaps we need not entirely rule out the possibility that the unknown causes are related to the death as something that is not known, or assimilable to cognition. This would suggest that the lines pose an alternative to the model of loss as a known cause, an alternative represented also by the peculiar pairing of the figure of communion with that of "props." To describe the mother—or is it just her body, the breasts?—as "props," is to make of her support an artificial structure, part of an edifice which the soul manipulates for its own architectonic purposes. Props have no place in a dynamic of life and death, but are rather part of a mechanical operation of placement and removal. The mother becomes something like the joints of a skeletal structure; the sustaining "spirit" of this "building," in spite of the later "communion," does not seem to be a very holy ghost. The cognitive uncertainty of the death is thus associated with a figurative uncertainty in the language, in which the figure of communion is placed side by side with a mechanical language of joining and propping, the latter having the effect of disjoining the figure of the breast from the mother, and the mother from nature. This disrupts the passage from maternal props to natural properties, and even from the mother to what is proper to her, leaving us with the unexpected figure of a mother with a prosthetic breast.

The uncertainty of the "unknown causes" is evident also in the passage in Book Four in which knowledge is introduced in a negative mode. The observer, as we recall, "now is crossed by gleam / Of his own image, by a sunbeam now, / And wavering motions sent he knows not whence." The perceptual certainty of the "now, now" is echoed by a "knows not" that serves less as a sign of mere ignorance than a warning of a knowledge not only unknowable but also better left unknown, an ominous "no, no." [14] Indeed, in Book Five, the figuration of this passage finds a "literal" repetition that is far less solacing than the scene with the mother. This is the well-known episode of the drowned man, which is also a search for a recognizable face, in a lake referred to again as a "breast" (1. 440):

> some looked
> In passive expectation from the shore,
> While from a boat others hung o'er the deep,
> Sounding with grappling irons and long poles.
> At last the dead man . . . bolt upright
> Rose, with his ghastly face.
>
> (1850, 444–50)

A critical emphasis on motion, or passing, is once again apparent in the contrast of "passive" looking and the "sounding" motions of those who "hung o'er the deep." [15] The image of a face is replaced here, however, by a real dead face which, presumably, stops this motion. What is disturbing is that the motion is *not* entirely stopped: the dead man "rises" as if by his own power, making his ghastly face rather ghostly. The breast of water on which he floats serves in this case as a prop that supports and makes the dead appear living: it propagates, so to speak, the appearance of a living motion. This complicates the opposition of motion and stillness as figurative and literal meaning, specifically in relation to the knowledge of a death.

Indeed, the propping function of the water suggests that the "props" of the mother have not, in fact, been entirely removed, and that the "unknowability" of their movement concerns precisely this remaining. The remainder of the props in some way disturbs the balance of literal and figurative meaning, and hence the cognitive assimilation of loss.

This question is raised again in Books Four and Seven, where props reappear in connection with the other ghastly figures of the Discharged Soldier "propped" by a milestone and the Blind Beggar "propped against a wall."[16] Both characters, like the drowned man, are associated with the stopping of a movement, but in the place of a physical motion each of them provides the story of his life. The peculiarity of this story, in the case of the soldier, is characterized by the "indifference" with which he tells it. While this indifference designates the emotional condition of being "unmoved," it also describes the process of storytelling, or listening, as the subsumption of a series of articulated differences in the appearance of a narrative "movement." In the later description of the Blind Beggar, this peculiar relation of difference and indifference becomes the disjunction between the "sightless eyes" of the man and the written paper on his chest—or breast—which he cannot read, and which yet makes possible, for the poet, a story of his own.[17] The disturbance of the literal-figurative relation seems to concern a shift to another relation, between the articulation of differences in reading, and the meaningful whole of the narrative movement.

The association of the breast with reading intimated by the scene of the poet reading the paper on the beggar's chest suggests that the Blessed Babe scene, considered in this context, might have something to tell us about the "remainder," which, associated with props, connects the reading of narratives with the relation to the mother. The problem of difference and indifference, furthermore, resituates this passage in terms of the polemic against empirical philosophy which introduces it, and in which a prop once again surfaces. The error attributed here

(11. 208 ff.) to philosophy—the confusion of things "which we perceive" with things "which we have made"—is not altogether unlike the activity of reading a series of signs as a sign of life. The similarity of Wordsworth's polemic to Locke's comments (in the *Conduct of the Understanding*) on distinction ("the perception of a difference that nature has placed in things") and division ("making a division where there is yet none"), which associate their confusion with the art of disputing, also suggests that this error is shared by philosophy and poetry, uniting science or empirical philosophy, the "prop of our infirmity," with the "prop of our affections." Thus the Blessed Babe passage, while appearing to offer itself as an alternative to the errors of mere philosophical quibbling, examines more profoundly the conditions of its own narration, or the problem of marking the difference between difference and indifference.[18]

Turning briefly, once again, to this passage, we see that the problem of narrative "distinction and division" rests, as might be expected, on the figure of passage:

> Blessed the infant babe—
> For with my best conjectures I would trace
> The progress of our being—blest the babe
> Nursed in his mother's arms, the babe who sleeps
> Upon his mother's breast, who, when his soul
> Claims manifest kindred with an earthly soul,
> Doth gather passion from his mother's eye.
> Such feelings pass into his torpid life
> Like an awakening breeze, and hence his mind . . .
> Is prompt and watchful, eager to combine
> In one appearance all the elements
> And parts of the same object, else detached
> And loth to coalesce.
>
> (1805, 237–50)

The movement from "passions," to "passing," to combining elements "in one appearance" suggests that the substitution we earlier saw beginning with the mother's death in fact has its origins here. The negative side of "passion" in its Christian con-

notations strengthens this suggestion. But what does it mean
to situate this negativity in the relation with the living mother?
If we read the figure of passion in relation to the "communion"
after the mother's death, we can perhaps understand passion as
a sort of prefiguration of loss, a figure for the mortality of a
soul that has entered the empirical world. But this does not account for the odd phrase "gathers passion from his mother's
eye." However, an alteration in the 1850 version, and included
in at least one edition of the 1805 version,[19] provides another
link between these lines and the death passage, one which depends not on the figurative—or literal—meaning of the lines,
but on a syntactical mark. This version adds an exclamation
point after "mother's eye" as well as at the end of the line describing the removal of the props.[20] If passion can be read as a
function of life and death, the "gathering" of passion is closer
to the more arbitrary combining of two passages on the basis of
a syntactical repetition. As opposed to the substitutive "combining in one appearance," which works figuratively to assimilate
visual perception to language, this "gathering" is a throwing
together (like the poet's "con-jectures"), a bonding which, like
a syntax, is not itself a function of meaning but rather the prop
upon which meaning leans, and with which it is immediately
confused. The repetition of the exclamation point in these passages foregrounds those aspects of language, such as syntax
and punctuation, which articulate "prior" to, or as the condition of possibility of, meaningful discourse, and which remain
to disturb the balance of syntax and semantics, literal and figurative meaning.[21]

This second story of the child at the breast, however, cannot exactly be considered *a* story the way the other can; for the
prop is, from the beginning, double. The mother can be considered a prop in two ways: as an empirical body, a "breast,"
she is the empirical element necessary for the beginning of a
life story (just as, according to Kant, experience is necessary
for, although not the origin of, conceptual activity). To this extent she is the prop of nature, the "prop of our infirmity," per-

haps. But to the extent that the mother's body is used, or manipulated, for articulating a story, that is, marked and read as the "mother," it has become purely part of an articulated structure, the skeletal hinge of a syntactical chain. Insofar as "she" is the latter, or is the name given to the latter, the mother is no longer *present* in any empirical sense and can thus be said to be "removed"; but since this articulation is, from the "beginning," necessary for the relation of affection, the mother has to be a "prop," and hence "removed," in order to be accessible to experience in the first place. We might say that, as a prop, the mother is not experienced, but read; and while this is necessary for her to become a "mother," or "kin," to this extent she is also not a "natural relation."[22] If the scene of the poet reading the paper on the beggar's chest recalls the "original" relation with the mother, it is only because in order to nurse *his mother's* breast the babe first has to read it.[23]

To speak of this activity in terms of "propping" is, however, to have shifted into the realm of figuration, which then encompasses, if somewhat uncomfortably, other figures such as that of passion and communion. This shift, which allows for the totalizing movement of self-recognition, the "combining in one appearance" that is described for example in Book Four, is marked by the word *eye*, which could be said to designate the confusion of reading and seeing, or to figure reading as something that is peculiar to the ocular sense organ. If we understand the two stories, of passion and of propping, in terms of the relation of figuration and articulation, we must recognize that this distinction can also be understood in terms of figuration itself, as assimilable to sense perception, and as unassimilable to it. This suggests that the mother, while designating an empirical beginning, can also be read as the figure of an "origin" that cannot be located temporally or spatially and leaves its traces over and over again in syntactical remainders. Understanding this repetitive, "originary" moment in terms of the relation of articulation and figuration, it might be possible to read certain histories of self-knowledge, such as those of Wordsworth and Freud, as the narrativization of a less *knowable* relation, which may even be disruptive to the narrative as such. We might think of this, for example in Freud, in terms of the relation of trace and symbol in the trauma theory, which could prove interesting in the understanding of Freud's theory of sexuality. It is not possible to elaborate at this point on the implications of this reading, but only to suggest it as a possible approach to the questions raised in the beginning of this chapter.

How this would affect the concept of repression is uncertain. How it affects the concept of death in *The Prelude* is evident in the reference to the babe's activity as "mute dialogues with my mother's heart," which echoes the description, in Book Five, of the poet standing "mute" before the Boy of Winander's grave. To the extent that the poet reads the story of a life in the inscription on a gravestone, the babe has, with its first "articulate prattle," already written the mother's epitaph on her body. But to read this is also for the babe to read its own birth certificate, the beginning of its self-knowledge as a historical being. It is our task, then, to follow in Freud's texts the traces of such a double movement, and perhaps also to hear in his frequent reference to the mother's role in emotional life Wordsworth's double eulogy, in *The Prelude,* for his mother:

> Early died
> My honoured mother, she who was the *heart*
> And *hinge* of all our learnings and our loves.
>
> (1805, V.256–58, italics added)

3

THE FORCE OF EXAMPLE

Kant's Symbols

 Recent literary theory has raised objections to what appears to be an overexclusive concern with "language" in poststructuralist literary criticism. While literary texts are linguistic constructs, so critics have argued, language itself must be seen in a historical and social context. Literary criticism must therefore turn to fields in the social sciences, such as sociology and history, to provide an understanding of the nonlinguistic elements that surround and in part determine the language of the texts that literary criticism studies. Otherwise it will be at risk of wrongly imperializing the nonlinguistic world with what happens to be its particular object of interest, and consequently limiting the understanding of its own object as well.[1]

This objection is important because it raises a question that was at one time not limited to literary criticism but pertained to the nonmathematical sciences in general, that is, whether and in what way they give access to a knowledge of the empirical world. The form in which the recent objections concerning literary criticism are raised, however, locates the problem, implicitly, in the *object* of study; the error is seen to be contingent upon the linguistic makeup of the objects with which literary criticism is concerned. If we turn to the philosophical texts in which the question of discursive theoretical knowledge was originally posed, however, the problem does not begin with the nature of the object but with the nature of the theory itself. Indeed, the entire project of Kant's critical philosophy could be considered an attempt to discover whether a philosophy based on principles not simply derived from either mathematics or empirical evidence could provide any systematic knowledge whatsoever. In order to provide any knowledge of objects, philosophy had to be able to systematize itself, as rigorously as mathematics. Whether discursive theory could say something about the world depended on what it could say about itself. If we are to remember the questions raised again today in the field of literary theory we must first ask, not "What can a theory of literature know?" but "What can theory know?"

Kant is a good place to examine this question not only because he first asked it in this form, but because his critical philosophy has seemed particularly dependent upon nondiscursive science, specifically Newtonian physics.[2] Kant's answer to what philosophy can know, that is, has seemed to be closely linked to what Newtonian physics knows, and hence it appears itself circumscribed by an empirical/historical determinant. But it turns out that in Kant the particular concept that will eventually allow theory to know is the concept of self-limitation, which is best thought of in terms of symbolic language. To some extent, then, an examination of the relation between critical philosophy and nondiscursive science will reveal that in order for philosophy to systematize itself it will first have to symbolize itself in its own self-knowledge.

In the preface to the second edition of the *Critique of Pure Reason,* Kant describes the dilemma of a metaphysics fallen into disrepute in the face of the successes of mathematics and natural science. The success of the mathematical sciences, Kant suggests, is that they base their method on an act of rational self-reflection in which the object is recognized as a representation of reason.[3] The structure of scientific method is one of self-recognition; what reason sees in nature is precisely itself. Reason thus makes progress in mathematics and physics because through their objects—number and empirical nature—rational thought learns more and more about itself. In this context, the failure of metaphysics contains a peculiar irony, since it is the science concerned most directly with what would seem purely rational objects, that is, "mere concepts." In the one science in which reason would seem to have the best chance of confronting itself directly, it is the least successful; reason is somehow furthest from itself when it is potentially nearest.[4] It has thus come to recognize itself first of all in the sciences in which it must detour through sensible intuition, through an "application" of concepts to objects, and hence through something exterior to the concept as such.

The successes of the sciences that Kant describes in the second preface are more than a point of comparison for metaphysical failure; in the context in which he is writing, they would seem, indeed, to be the very cause of the metaphysical dilemma. In 1687 Newton had published the laws of motion in his *Principia,* sparking a series of debates that centered upon what might be considered the central innovation of the *Principia:* Newton's assertion that the movement of massive bodies separated in space could be described in terms of an attractive force exerted by these bodies on each other. The concept of attractive force was a breakthrough because it provided a way of explaining and testing the Copernican astronomy, which had no way of proving its claims over the Ptolemaic system.[5] But the strength of the concept of gravitation for physics was also its bane for philosophy. The problem that inspired the commentary of Locke, Leibniz, Hume, and others was that while the Newtonian formulas worked effectively in predicting physical phenomena, and seemed to be inductively justified—that is, while the *law* of gravitation seemed perfectly "true"—the *concept* of attractive force as a physical event, an attraction across empty space, made no sense in rational terms. "Action at a distance," or "gravitation," seemed to be a speculative "hypothesis" or in Leibniz's terms an "occult quality." Thus the concept of gravitation seemed to achieve scientific (mathematical-em-

pirical) description at the cost of philosophical understanding.
The laws of the empirical world were beyond the grasp of
a philosophical understanding that was not as rigorous as a
mathematically governed system.[6]
   It was the innovation of critical philosophy to question
the attempt to model philosophical understanding on mathematics or scientific law, by rigorously examining the principle
of their difference. Instead of asking "How can philosophy
understand the world?" criticism would ask "How is philosophical understanding different from (mathematical-) scientific understanding?" Thus in the "Doctrine of Method" of the
first *Critique,* Kant defines the rigor of philosophical method
through its difference from mathematics:

> Mathematics and philosophy, although in natural science they
> do, indeed, go hand in hand, are none the less so completely
> different, that the procedure of the one can never be imitated by
> the other.
>   The exactness of mathematics rests upon definitions, axioms
> and demonstrations . . . whereas philosophy consists precisely
> in knowing its limits.[7]

If the rigor of mathematics consists in the complete and autonomous definition of its objects, the rigor of philosophy consists
in the determination, not of an object (including itself), but of
its own "limits." What it knows is precisely the ways in which it
cannot know objects directly or completely. Such a negative
knowledge is not, therefore, a knowledge of an object as such
but rather of its own *relation* to an object. To know its limits is
to know that its knowledge of an object is always relational, a
relation between the object and itself. This produces a kind of
double limitation: on the one hand, philosophy will know that
it can never know objects in themselves, that is, that it "can
never transcend the limits of possible experience";[8] the "transcendental" concepts will always only provide knowledge of
the relation between themselves and an empirical "given." On
the other hand, the knowledge of this limitation must itself re-

main limited: it must be understood in terms of a relation to something that is not knowledge. This "something" is precisely the supersensible, which is not grasped by "knowing" (*erkennen*) but only posited by "thinking" (*denken*).[9] What critical philosophy ultimately knows, then, is simply this relation between knowing and thinking: philosophy remains suspended between a direct knowledge of empirical objects and any knowledge of the supersensible, which it can only "think." In this principle of suspension, the difference between mathematics and philosophy has been converted from a flaw hindering metaphysical progress into the very ground of its rigor.

Kant thus establishes a link between purely conceptual knowledge and the natural sciences on the basis of the principle of limitation. That is, it is the rigorous negativity of conceptual self-reflection that links it to the rigors of mathematical calculation. Indeed, the relation between natural science and philosophy in Kant's system could be defined in terms of what they *don't* know: while natural science describes the world directly, it gives up the possibility of *understanding* it, and philosophy, while it *understands*, cannot understand *the world*. On this basis Kant develops the elaborate system called the "architectonic," divided between (1) the purely "transcendental" laws, which provide the "conditions of possibility" of experience—for example the law that "every change must have a cause"; (2) the "metaphysical laws," which are based on the transcendental laws as well as on mathematics and empirical "givens," and explain the fundamental features of the material world—for example the law that "every change of matter must have an external cause," that is, Newton's first law of motion;[10] and (3) the physical laws, which concern more specific characteristics of the physical world.[11] Thus, in the case of force, "metaphysics" (which is basically Newtonian physics) need only explain the law mathematically and be able to test and prove its effects experimentally, while philosophy need only explain the transcendental *conditions* for knowing the concept—that is, the law of causality. The centrality of the enigma of force in the most rigorous of natural sciences is linked to the centrality of the negative self-reflection of conceptual knowledge in critical philosophy.

Certain problems have arisen, however, concerning this close correspondence of natural science and philosophy, which would seem to be the triumph of critical rigor. Many readers of Kant have suggested that what determines the structure of the system is not, in fact, a conceptual principle, but an analogy with the already constituted science of physics, upon which Kant based his conception of philosophy. The most rigorous of defenders of the conceptual independence of the system, Gerd Buchdahl, while insisting on the *general* applicability of the transcendental laws to empirical "givens" (or to "experience"), also notes that in the relation to metaphysics there is "the working of something like analogy," and he concludes that Newtonian physics to some extent "historically conditioned the general construction of the architectonic."[12] Ultimately, then, in spite of its pretensions, the critical philosophy would seem incapable of wresting itself from basically empirical determinants. What philosophical theory knows, in Kant, would still depend on, and to that extent be secondary to, what empirical science knows.

Buchdahl's use of the word *analogy* calls attention to the way in which Newtonian physics, or more specifically the relation between force and motion, seems to serve as the model for all conceptual relations *within* the transcendental system. The entire concept of relation seems to be modeled, in fact, on the concept of the *event* and its *effects*, or the nonphenomenal occurrence and its representation. Thus, in the first *Critique*, the pure transcendental concepts that Kant defines in his "Table of Categories" are divided into the "mathematical" and "dynamical," with the three "Analogies of Experience" in the latter corresponding closely to the three laws of motion in the "Metaphysics." The distinction between the mathematical and dynamical categories is itself reiterated in the larger division between the *Analytic* and the *Dialectic* of the first *Critique*, or the analysis of what philosophy can *know* and what it can just *think*. And once again, the division between Analytic and Dialectic in the theoretical realm is repeated in the division between theoretical philosophy and practical philosophy, or the branches of philosophy concerned with the knowledge of nature and with human action. Criticism's own model for its negative self-knowledge would thus appear to be that of a knowledge turned upon itself by the action of a force heterogeneous to, but not separable from, this motion.[13] The entire conceptual structure of critical philosophy, that is, would appear to be *taken over* from Newtonian physics and thus to look to the empirical world both for the basis of its conceptual structures (modeling its own laws on the laws of physics) and the basis of its own self-representation (representing itself on the model of empirical events). Hence the very knowledge of the *difference* from empirical law which forms the basis of critical thought appears to be, itself, modeled on an empirical event, and the knowledge provided by the discursive theory appears to be traceable, once again, to an *empirical* determinant.

It would be useful, however, before jumping to conclusions, to look somewhat more closely at the actual place in which Kant elaborates, within his critical system, on the principles and foundations of Newtonian physics, the *Metaphysical Foundations of Natural Science*. In the preface to this work Kant himself comments on the curious dependence of transcendental philosophy on metaphysical law. He sees this dependent relation in the "example":

> It is indeed very remarkable (but cannot here be thoroughly entered into) that general metaphysics in all cases where it requires [*Beispiele*] (intuitions) in order to provide meaning [*Bedeutung*] for its pure concepts of the understanding must always take them from the general doctrine of body, i.e., from the form and principles of external intuition [*äussere Anschauung*]; and if these examples are not at hand in their entirety it gropes [*herumtappe*], uncertain and trembling, among mere meaning-

> less concepts . . . and so a separate metaphysics of corporeal na-
> ture does excellent and indispensable service to general meta-
> physics, inasmuch as the former provides examples [*Beispiele*]
> (cases in concreto) in which to realize the concepts and proposi-
> tions of the latter (properly, transcendental philosophy), i.e., to
> give to a mere form of thought sense and meaning [*Sinn und
> Bedeutung*].[14]

Kant is concerned here with the fact that transcendental philosophy, as a purely formal structure, a "mere form of thought"
(*einer blossen Gedankenform*), depends on something outside of
the concept, or "examples," for its "meaning" (*Bedeutung*).[15]
What surprises Kant, however, is not just the dependence of
the "form" on any illustrative "intuition," but rather the dependence of the form specifically on "*external* intuition" or "the
general doctrine of body." External intuition, here, is not just a
content that gives meaning to the conceptual form, but itself
has a "form" and "principles" in the science of dynamics: it is
another "form" which is the meaning of the "mere form" of
thought. The need for something "external" to thought is thus,
here, different from the need for "experience" in general which
Kant emphasizes throughout the first *Critique:* it is another
kind of externality represented by the dependence of the form
of transcendental philosophy on the form of Newtonian science, a doubling of form and form.

   This doubling reappears in the use of the word *external* in
the *Foundations* as a whole, in which it comes to stand for two
different kinds of relation. In the preface, Kant first speaks of
the doctrine of body as the science that concerns objects that
"affect" the "external senses."[16] Here matter, defined as motion, is "external" insofar as it is "given" to the concept; it is
that empirical "given" to which the concept must always stand
in relation. Yet matter as motion, as Kant writes of it in the
main work, is defined by "external relations" in a much more
formal sense: the motion of a thing is said to be "the change of
its external relations to a given space."[17] In this case, "external"

refers to relations that can be calculated mathematically. Thus matter, insofar as it affects the "external senses," is that which is *given* to them; but, insofar as it is determined by "external relations," it is that which can be calculated. "External" thus seems to mean both the "philosophical" relation that defines the negativity of conceptual self-reflection and the purely mathematical relation of number. The peculiarity of the metaphysical "example" thus lies in the joining of these two kinds of "external" relations.

The joining of two external relations, it turns out, becomes the very principle of the central law of the *Foundations*. In the "second law of mechanics," Kant reformulates Newton's first law (which, with the other two, gave rise to the theory of gravitation) in terms of the transcendental law of causality. It is thus here that he joins the central principles of transcendental philosophy and metaphysics:

Proposition
Second law of mechanics: Every change of matter has an external cause [*eine äussere Ursache*]. (Every body remains in its state of rest or motion in the same direction and with the same velocity unless it is compelled by an external cause to forsake this state).

Proof
(In universal metaphysics there is laid down the proposition that every change has a cause; here there is only to be proved of matter that its change must always have an external cause.) Matter as mere object of the external senses [*aüsserer Sinne*] has no other determinations than those of external relations in space [*der äusseren Verhältnisse im Raume*] and hence undergoes no changes except by motion. With regard to such change, insofar as it is an exchange of one motion with another, or of motion with rest, and vice versa, a cause of such change must be found (according to the principle of metaphysics). But this cause cannot be internal [*innerlich*], for matter has no absolutely internal determinations and grounds of determination.

> Hence all change of matter is based upon an external cause (i.e.,
> a body remains etc.).[18]

In the "Proposition" Kant reformulates Newton's first law in
metaphysical terms in order to show its relation to transcendental principles. In this reformulation, the difference between
the "second law of mechanics" and the transcendental law of
causality lies primarily in the addition of the word *external*. Its
significance is also emphasized by the fact that the reiteration
of the law in stricter Newtonian form (in parentheses) replaces
Newton's "forces" (*viribus*), with the phrase "external cause."[19]
Thus the entire weight of the law, insofar as it articulates metaphysical and transcendental principles, rests on the notion of
the "external." In the "Proof," moreover, this term can be seen
to involve a double meaning, referring both to the definition of
matter and to the explanation of its change. For matter is defined, first of all, in terms of "external relations," in which "external" means purely mathematical calculability. But in the application of the transcendental law to matter, "external" refers
to that which *affects* "external relations," that is, to that which
is external to external relations. This latter externality cannot
be discovered empirically but only by the use of a transcendental concept. Thus at this moment, in the phrase "external
cause," "external" is no longer precisely mathematical (or empirical) but conceptual. The example of force as an "external
cause" expresses, therefore, the precise point of articulation between metaphysical and transcendental law in terms of a principle of double relation or "externality."

In the "Observation" following the proof, Kant comments on the centrality of this law for natural philosophy. The
doubleness of the external as mathematical and as empirical
now is given a different name, that of "lifelessness":

> This mechanical law alone must be called the law of inertia [*lex
> inertiae*]; the law that every action has an equal and opposite
> reaction cannot bear this name. For the latter says what matter
> does, but the former only what it does not do, and this is better

adapted to the expression of inertia. The inertia of matter is and signifies [*bedeutet*] nothing but its lifelessness [*Leblosigkeit*], as matter in itself. Life [*Leben*] means the capacity of a substance to determine itself to act from an internal principle . . . Now, we know of no other principle of a substance to change its state but desire . . . but these determining grounds and actions do not at all belong to the representations of the external senses and hence also not to the determinations of matter as matter. Therefore, all matter as such is lifeless [*leblos*]. The proposition of inertia says so much and no more . . . The possibility of a natural science proper rests entirely upon the law of inertia (along with the law of the permanence of substance). The opposite of this, and therefore the death of all natural philosophy [*der Tod aller Naturphilosophie*], would be hylozoism.[20]

The significance of the law of inertia within the critical system is emphasized here in terms of its purely negative character: much like transcendental philosophy itself, it is concerned less with positive assertion than with a kind of limitation. It is this negativity that would essentially bind the metaphysical law to the transcendental one: the expression of what matter does *not* do corresponds to the expression of what transcendental concepts cannot know. This not knowing, moreover, is specifically defined as a suspension of all comparisons between matter, or motion and its causes, to human life: the power of the law to suspend understanding and confine itself to calculation lies in its resistance to any figurations that compare matter with the mind or personify it, as in "hylozoism"; matter "in itself," as the cause of its own movements, remains utterly outside this sort of comprehension. Kant clearly has in mind here the various attempts to explain attractive force in terms of a kind of inner life of matter, but it is significant that he carefully elides the word *force* and uses instead the word *lifelessness*. "Life*less*" (leb*los*) is itself a negative determination which encompasses both the externality of matter as "external relations" in space and the externality of material cause: the *event* of force as a purely calculable and incomprehensible occurrence can only be understood negatively by saying that it is *not* a living action. The word *lifeless* thus represents the full negativity which serves as the hinge for the different parts of the system, the "giving up" of a claim to understanding (in the case of natural science) or of direct knowledge (in the case of transcendental philosophy). "Lifelessness" expresses, that is, the relational quality of all conceptual knowledge, which knows in its object only its own *relation* to a "something" that is not fully determined.

The rigor of this use of the word *lifeless* for a purely conceptual negativity gives way further on in the passage, however, to a different kind of language, when Kant informs us that the opposite of *inertia*, or hylozoism, "would be the death of all philosophy." The interest of this phrase is not just that it is meant figuratively, but that the figurative meaning turns on the notion of lifelessness, which is now characterized positively, and more humanly, as "death" (*Tod*). If *matter* is characterized as purely inhuman, philosophy dies a very personal death, one which establishes a specific figurative relation between the two: the life of matter is the death of philosophy; the lifelessness of matter is the life of philosophy. The force of the chiasmus compels the reading of a narrative into the relation between matter (or natural law) and philosophy, which gives the "lifelessness" of matter a more personal cast: matter dies, it would appear, *so that* philosophy can have life. The negativity which mediates between metaphysical and transcendental law is no longer purely conceptual but takes the form of a story: what mediates, here, is a death, a sacrifice of one life in the service of another. This story sounds familiar, and can be heard, perhaps, in the original law, when we read that matter only "suffers" (*erleidet*) change by means of external causes: when matter suffers death (*erleidet den Tod*) for philosophy, it mediates between concept and empirical law as Christ's death (*das Leiden Christi*) mediates between fallen man and God. The mediation of limit-thinking has shifted from a purely negative conceptual structure to a story in which negativity is represented in terms of a death.

Our discovery of a narrative dimension in the *Foundations* might seem mere speculation, but Kant's figuration is not confined to the single instance of the "Observation"; it does not seem, that is, to be simply the effect of a moment of imaginative excess. It was already present, in some sense, in the passage on "examples" in the preface, in which, we recall, it was said that without examples philosophy "gropes, uncertain and trembling, among meaningless concepts." The personification of philosophy here—based on the same word, *gropes* (*herumtappe*), that is used to characterize it in the preface to the second edition of the first *Critique*—suggests that the relation between philosophy and metaphysics is less like a conceptual relation than like a power relation.[21] The dependence of transcendental philosophy on metaphysics, in the "example," is dramatized as the dependence of a master on the "indispensable services [*Dienst*]" of its servant (in Hegel, notably, *Dienst* is the word used to describe the function of the slave in the master-slave section of the *Phenomenology of Spirit*, where death will also be a mediating term). The mediation provided by the example can, therefore, be understood in narrative terms. And this narrative is closely linked to the narrative told in the second law, the story of the death of matter for the life of philosophy, or the "falling" (for the effect of force is the fall of motion) which makes possible negative critical self-consciousness. Force is a kind of death, an occurrence *in critical thinking* which makes possible the mediation of empirical and conceptual thought and which can no longer be understood in purely empirical terms. Force, or death, would appear to be the narrative figure *of* the mediation provided by the example, of the relational structure which relates critical knowledge to itself.[22]

The problem that metaphysics presents to transcendental philosophy cannot be understood, therefore, in terms of the dependence of the conceptual model on an empirical law *outside* of it, or the grounding of the "analogy" in an empirical necessity.[23] Dependence, and outsideness or externality, are, as we have seen, understandable also within a narrative that robs them of any purely empirical meaning. The extra "externality" of force, or what seems to threaten purely conceptual thought, must also be understood in other terms, as a problem that arises from within the very conceptualization of limitation itself. That is, the example, as the structure of relation, first reflects back upon the concept of relation in the notion of the "limitation" of reason as a relation between the sensible and supersensible realms. The best place to turn in order to try to understand this problem better will thus be the part of the system in which the concept of limitation is most carefully discussed, the section called "On the Determination of the Limits of Pure Reason" in Kant's summary of critical philosophy, *Prolegomena to Any Future Metaphysics*. It is also here, in the discussion of the concept of the limit, that we will rediscover the figure, or story, of death. The problems raised by the *Foundations*—the question of the *basis* of transcendental thinking in relation to the empirical world—will thus be best addressed by a look at the determination of the "limit."

The discussion of the limit-concept is an attempt to explain, precisely, how self-limitation must be understood in terms of a relation, specifically a relation to the supersensible. In an earlier section, Kant had indicated that the necessity of understanding a relation to the supersensible is implied in all rigorous conceptions of empirical knowledge. He calls this other realm to which knowledge is related, implicit in the relation between concepts and empirical law, the "realm of mere ideas." Not surprisingly what necessitates the thinking of these ideas is exemplified here by attractive force:

> The objects which are given us by experience are in many respects incomprehensible, and many questions to which the law of nature leads us when carried beyond a certain point (though still quite conformably to the laws of nature) admit of no answer. An example is the question: Why do material things attract one another? But if we entirely quit nature or, in pursuing its combinations, exceed all possible experience, and so enter

the realm of mere Ideas, we cannot then say that the object is incomprehensible. . . . Although an absolute whole of experience is impossible, the Idea of a whole of knowledge according to principles must impart to our knowledge a kind of unity, that of a system, without which it is nothing but piecework.[24]

If we think of the "incomprehensibility" of experience as it is described here in terms of the structure of the metaphysical example, we can see that Kant is concerned with the grounding of the kind of negative knowledge that transcendental philosophy provides through its relational thinking. As we saw, the power of the system to establish always only a knowledge of a relation, rather than of an object itself, is expressed in the giving up, by transcendental philosophy, of any full knowledge of attractive force, allowing it to represent only the necessity of the relation of the concept of causality to what is "given" to it empirically. Here Kant reminds us that this negative relation is itself made possible only in relation to another relation, the concept of the limitation of the sensible by the supersensible. It is this relation, we recall, which says not only that knowledge is limited *to* the sensible, but that the knowledge *of* the limitation is itself limited, is not a full, transparent knowledge of knowledge. Here Kant emphasizes that this final limitation of limitation is precisely what permits the limit-concept to provide a principle of epistemological closure, to make critical knowledge into a *system*. The establishment of a relation to supersensible ideas—the kind of thinking Kant calls *denken*—is what permits critical knowledge to *know*, rigorously, that it cannot know itself fully.

The section on the determination of limits is thus concerned with explaining how the concept of the limit establishes a relation to something outside of knowledge. Kant focuses the discussion on the difference between this relational concept and the "mere negations" of Humean skepticism, which is, like all dogmatic (i.e., noncritical) philosophy, still aimed at the direct knowledge of objects, including knowledge itself. Kant thus contrasts the different kinds of negativity in skepticism and criticism in terms of the "boundaries" established by Hume and the "limits" established by criticism:

> Our principles, which limit the use of reason to possible experience, might . . . become transcendent and the limits of our reason be set up as limits of the possibility of things in themselves (as Hume's *Dialogues* may illustrate) if a careful critique did not guard the limits of our reason with respect to its empirical use and set a limit to its pretensions. . . .
>
> . . . In all limits [*Grenzen*] there is something positive (for example, a surface is the limit of corporeal space, and is therefore itself a space; a line is a space, which is the limit of the surface, a point the limit of the line, but yet always a place in space), but boundaries contain mere negations . . . The question now is, What is the attitude of our reason in this connection of what we know with what we do not, and never shall, know? This is an actual connection of a known thing with one quite unknown (and which will always remain so), and though what is unknown should not become in the least more known—which we cannot even hope—yet the concept of this connection must be definite and capable of being rendered distinct. . . .
>
> We must therefore think [*denken*] an immaterial being, a world of understanding, and a Supreme Being. . . .
>
> But as we can never know [*erkennen*] these beings of understanding as they are in themselves, that is, as definite, yet must assume them as regards the sensible world and connect them with it by reason, we are at least able to think [*denken*] this connection by means of such concepts as express their relation to the world of sense.[25]

The "mere negation" of skepticism, Kant implies in these passages, would claim to *know* the world as empty of supersensible beings, because it takes the knowledge of its own limits as absolute, that is, because it believes that the knowledge of limits is not itself limited, i.e., is itself supersensible. Kant thus implicitly points to a contradiction in skepticism, that in *negating* all supersensible knowledge, in claiming to *know* that we can only know the empirical world, it relies on the supersensible nature of its *self-knowledge*. The critical insistence on positing a relation to the supersensible thus preserves negative self-knowledge from erroneously attributing a supersensible status to itself. It maintains a completely rigorous negativity by precisely *positing* or "thinking" a *relation* to the supersensible, rather than claiming to know either the presence or absence of this supersensible world. The "thinking" of the relation thus remains, primarily, self-reflexive, because what it says is only that self-knowledge *must* limit itself in a certain way. It says, that is, that criticism can *know* where its knowledge of knowledge stops—it can know the difference between knowing and thinking. It is the rigor of this distinction which permits the negativity of limit-knowledge to produce a closed and systematic philosophy.

The question Kant insists must be answered, however, is precisely *how* we can conceive of a relation that is "thought" rather than known. Kant's discussion of this problem will center, again, on a debate with Hume, concerning one specific question: whether or not "God," as a supersensible being, can be thought in a fully critical (i.e., relational) manner. Hume has insisted, Kant says, that God can only be thought "anthropomorphically," that is, by a transfer of qualities from the sensible world (specifically, understanding), and hence only erroneously, as a fiction of a supersensible being which is in fact thought entirely in sensible terms. For this reason Hume denies any truth to this representation. The skeptical "negation," Kant implies, thus rests on the belief that the representation of God is the attempt to *know* a supersensible object. Kant argues for another kind of representation:

> We stop at this limit [of experience] if we confine our judgment merely to the relation which the world may have to a Being whose very concept lies beyond all the knowledge which we can attain within the world. For we then do not attribute to the Supreme Being any of the properties in themselves by which we present objects of experience, and thereby avoid *dogmatic* anthropomorphism, but we attribute them to the relation of this Being to the world and allow ourselves a *symbolical* anthropomorphism, which in fact concerns language only and not the object itself.

> If I say that we are compelled to consider the world *as if* it
> were the work of a Supreme Understanding and Will, I really
> say nothing more than that a watch, a ship, a regiment, bears
> the same relation to the watchmaker, the shipbuilder, the com-
> manding officer as the world of sense (or whatever constitutes
> the substratum of this complex of appearances) does to the un-
> known, which I do not hereby know as it is in itself but as it is
> for me, that is, in relation to the world of which I am a part.[26]

Criticism, Kant suggests, permits a different way of representing God, which is not an attempt to know the supersensible,
but only a relation to it. The symbolic anthropomorphism does
not know, but, Kant implies, only thinks God. The difference
between skepticism, the most advanced of precritical philosophies, and criticism thus comes down to a difference between
two conceptions of anthropomorphism: dogmatic and symbolic—the representation that claims to know God and the
representation that claims only to know the relation to God.
With this distinction, Kant rests the entire weight of the critical
system—the full rigor of negative thinking—upon the capacity
for a certain kind of figuration. Or rather, upon the capacity of
criticism to know this figuration, that is, to distinguish between
the dogmatic and symbolic anthropomorphism, or to define the
symbol rigorously and completely. Since the symbol is, ultimately, the form in which thinking as such takes place, the
definition of the symbol will amount to the definition of the
distinction between knowing and thinking, and will thus constitute the most rigorous form of critical self-knowledge.

What is most significant in the definition of the symbolic
anthropomorphism is its self-reflexive capacity, made possible
by its purely relational character. Where the dogmatic anthropomorphism transfers properties from the world of sense to
God, Kant says, the symbolic anthropomorphism transfers only
relations. The symbol does not claim to know God, but only
something about our relation to this being. Since the knowledge of relation is, however, always a knowledge of knowledge,
the symbolic representation of the supersensible will also be a
reflection on the very establishing of the symbol, a symbol of

symbolic thinking. To think a symbolic relation is thus to represent the supersensible in terms of the very act of thinking which makes this representation possible. The symbol, that is, always remembers that it is, only, a symbol. It knows, one could say, that it posits. The symbol thus mediates between thinking and knowing, or the negativity of knowledge and the knowledge of that negativity. It is this self-mediation which gives rise to the possibility for criticism to distinguish itself over against skepticism, to distinguish between what is and what isn't a symbol. In the symbol, criticism first knows itself as what knows the difference between knowing and thinking. all other points of articulation in the system, such as the structure of exemplification, in which concepts reflect systematically on their own relation to their sensible objects, refer back to and are grounded upon this knowledge of thinking made possible by the symbol.

In defining the rigorous negativity of symbolic representation, however, Kant does not confine himself to a discussion of knowledge, but introduces another term as well, *language* (*die Sprache*): symbolic anthropomorphism, he says, "in fact concerns language only and not the object itself." The symbol, that is, reminds us not only that it is given by thought, but that it is given by language. It is not entirely clear what it means, here, to concern "language only," since the relation between the knowing/thinking distinction and language has not been defined. It would appear, however, that the introduction of this term indicates that the knowledge of the symbol cannot be contained completely by the terminology of thought. The thinking of the symbol has put a certain pressure on the critical argument that compels it to change its terms. At this point, the burden of the argument shifts from the attempt of critical thinking to know itself in symbols, to the attempt of critical language to represent itself in symbols. The unity of philosophy as a discursive science could be said to depend upon the possibility of this achievement.

This pressure on the argument concerning symbolic anthropomorphism, the sense that it requires a different kind of definition, is also felt in the following paragraph of the section, which provides a reformulation of the definition in terms of analogy: "Such a cognition is one of analogy and does not signify (as is commonly understood) an imperfect similarity of two things, but a perfect similarity between two quite dissimilar things."[27] The concept of analogy presumably represents the relational character, the self-reflexive capacity, of the symbol which has just been defined in the previous paragraphs. But the reformulation of the definition in terms of analogy brings with it new examples as well, as if the examples that have just been provided were not fully adequate. These examples are given in a footnote:

> There is, for example, an analogy between the juridical relation of human actions and the mechanical relation of moving forces . . . Here right and moving force are quite dissimilar things, but in their relation there is complete similarity . . . By means of such an analogy, I can obtain a notion of things which absolutely are unknown to me. For instance, as the promotion of the welfare of children (=a) is to the love of parents (=b), so the welfare of the human species (=c) is to that unknown character in God (=X), which we call love; not as if it had the least similarity to any human inclination, but because we can suppose its relation to the world to be similar to that which things of the world bear one another. But the concept of relation in this case is a mere category, namely, the concept of cause, which has nothing to do with sensibility.[28]

These examples differ from those in the main text in an interesting way: they are both linked closely to the categories that bind transcendental philosophy to metaphysics, that is, to the "analogies" linked to the three laws of motion. Thus they would appear to have a special status, a privileged place in the linkages that make up the system: they seem to correspond directly to the exemplary structure Kant finds so "remarkable" and which is also so troubling for the system. This would be the case, in particular, for the symbol that represents God's relation to man in terms of "love," since this is based on the concept of causality, and is thus the symbolic correlate of the example of inertia. The special status of this particular analogy in representing the symbol links the "remarkable" quality of the metaphysical example with the concept of analogy by which the self-reflexivity of symbolic language is represented. The narrative that emerges in the discussion of the law of inertia—the story of matter dying as a sacrifice to philosophy—would thus seem to point to this extra symbol in the footnote, the symbol of God's love.

The privileged place of this symbol seems to be represented, moreover, by its particular term of comparison, *love*, since love would appear to be the relation par excellence, in particular the love of a parent for a child. Yet the analogy remains somewhat unclear, because it is not so much the feeling of love that represents God's relation to man, but the causality of love, the causal relation of parental love to the child's welfare. Of all symbols to exemplify a causal analogy, love does not seem to be the most obvious. The impact of the figure of love in the symbol does not seem congruent, that is, with its strictly conceptual function as a relation of causality. As was the case in the example of inertia, the symbol of love seems to say more than the causal analogy suggests.

Kant indeed came back to this symbol ten years later in *Religion within the Limits of Reason Alone* (1793). Here again he discusses the necessity of representing supersensible ideas in sensible form, or "the personified idea of the good principle." In a footnote to this discussion he writes:

> It is indeed a limitation of human reason, and one which is ever inseparable from it, that we can conceive of no considerable moral worth in the actions of a personal being without representing that person, or his manifestation, in human guise. This is not to assert that such worth is in itself ($\kappa\alpha\tau'\dot{\alpha}\lambda\dot{\eta}\theta\varepsilon\omega\nu$) so conditioned, but merely that we must always resort to some analogy to natural existences to render supersensible qualities intelligible to ourselves . . . The Scriptures too accommodate themselves to this mode of representation when, in order to

make us comprehend the degree of God's love for the human race, they ascribe to Him the very highest sacrifice which a loving being can make, a sacrifice performed in order that even those who are unworthy may be made happy ("For God so loved the world . . ."); though we cannot indeed rationally conceive how an all-sufficient Being could sacrifice a part of what belongs to His state of bliss or rob Himself of a possession. Such is the *schematism of analogy*, with which (as a means of explanation) we cannot dispense. But to transform it into a *schematism of objective determination* (for the extension of our knowledge) is *anthropomorphism*, which has, from the moral point of view (in religion), most injurious consequences.[29]

The "schematism of analogy" that Kant attributes to Scripture here is an extension of the analogy discussed in the *Prolegomena:* there, God is represented symbolically by comparing his relation to man with the loving relation of parent and child; here, God's love for man is further represented in terms of the specific means by which this love is responsible for man's welfare (i.e., how God's love makes man "happy"). The analogy here, that is, explains the specific application of the causal category in the symbolic love relation. This causal efficacy of parental love is represented in terms of the operation of the sacrifice. It is God's sacrifice that permits "even those who are unworthy" to be made happy, that is, to be "saved." It is thus the specific structure of a sacrificial relation which permits the creation of the symbolic analogy between the phenomenal causal relation and the relation to the non-phenomenal being. That is, the structure of the symbol as a symbol of symbol is linked, not to *any* causal relation, but specifically to the sacrificial one. God's "love" has a privileged status as a symbol because it is defined by this structure.

The appropriateness of the sacrificial structure as the privileged symbol would seem to lie in its representation of the negative character of symbolic self-knowledge: the sacrifice is a loss suffered in the service of a gain.[30] In its broadest outlines in the footnote, this relation appears to be the loss suffered by

God, "robbing himself" of a possession, or sacrificing "part of his state of bliss," in order for man to be made "happy," or to achieve his own state of bliss. The sacrifice thus establishes a relation between God and man that is structured like a chiasmus, or an inverted analogy in which God and man exchange the properties of bliss and unhappiness through the agency of the sacrifice. Put in terms of the parent-child relationship of the earlier analogy, the chiasmus would appear as follows:

$$\frac{\text{Parent's bliss}}{\text{Child's unhappiness}} \times \frac{\text{Parent's unhappiness}}{\text{Child's bliss}}$$

This figure represents the negative relation between man and God (the bliss of one is the unhappiness of the other) as the principle of the unity between them. The symbol thus represents its own negativity in terms of a loss of the knowledge of God regained as the knowledge of the mere thinking of God, i.e., the knowledge of the limit.

If we examine the footnote carefully, however, the notion of the sacrifice does not appear to be entirely straightforward. The passage Kant cites from the Gospel of John reminds us that the loving sacrifice for the human child also involves another parent-child relationship:

> For God so loved the world, that he gave his only begotten Son, that whosoever believeth in him should not perish, but have everlasting life.
> For God sent not his Son into the world to condemn the world; but that the world through him might be saved.[31]

God's loving relation to man as his child depends on a relation to another child, the only true child. The parental relationship between God and man is mediated through the parental relationship between God and Christ. But in this mediating relation, the "sacrifice" is not the sacrifice *by* the parent but rather *of* the child: in sending his true son into the world so that the world might be saved "through" him, God is sending his first son to his death. The loving relation between parent and child

now depends upon a relation in which the parent sends another child to its death: man is only related to God as the
beloved child by being the second, foster child, the one that
comes after the first child is eliminated. If "parent and child"
represent the two-term relationship par excellence, the introduction of the Christ story suggests that there is an extra child
somewhere that had to be eliminated in order for parental love
to be established. The balance of the four terms of the analogy,
or of the two relations, depends on the suppression of another
relation which makes the establishment of the analogy possible
in the first place.

This other relation creates an imbalance which can be
thought of in terms of the chiastic structure of the sacrifice.
The extra child, or rather the death of the extra child, creates an
asymmetry in this structure, which must be reformulated now
not in terms of bliss and unhappiness but in terms of life and
death:

$$\frac{\text{Parent's life}}{\text{Child's death}} \times \frac{\text{Other child's death}}{\text{Child's life}}$$

The appearance of the other child's death in the analogy displaces the sacrifice from its position between the terms *God* and
man to a position "outside" of them, where it cannot be considered an act *of* either of them. Similarly, the agent of this
"death," or the other child, since it appears *only* in function *of*
its death, cannot be considered a child in any understandable
sense of the word (one could say that Christ, insofar as he appears here only as a child to be sacrificed for the parental love of
man, is already dead, and hence not a "beloved" child from the
beginning). The other relations within the analogy are thus
placed in relation to an "event" which cannot be understood as
either sensible or supersensible, an act or property of man or
of God. The negativity of this other relation—represented
as death—thus remains incomprehensible, since it cannot be
properly associated with either term: for man, it is God's death,
for God it is Christ's death. This other relation is not, there-

fore, comprehensible in terms of any kind of thought or knowable difference. If God's relation to the living child becomes comprehensible through the relation to the dead one, the latter cannot be considered a "relation" in any known sense of the term. The other's death, as it were, holds a place for man in the analogy; it opens up the relation in which a place will be reserved for man, even as it closes off the complete understanding of itself as a comprehensible event.[32]

This imbalance within the symbolic analogy, which both permits it to work and makes its complete self-closure impossible, indicates the impossibility for the symbol to represent itself adequately as language. What remains after the symbol has symbolized itself is always another term that is not contained within the symbolic structure. Thus the examples of the symbol given in the main text of the *Prolegomena* produce the examples in the footnote, and these generate other examples in other texts. The movement from symbol to symbol marks the excess of the language of the system in relation to its conceptualization, or the excessiveness of language as occurrence in relation to its self-representation. The division between thinking and knowing in the system, which takes the form of a self-closing structure, might thus be considered a displacement of the difference between event and representation in language, a difference that does not permit systematization as a structure. The attempt to contain this difference, this lag between the event and its representation, would produce, within the structure of the division between knowing and thinking, the narratives that emerge at points of articulation within the system. Thus, while the parent-child analogy in the first symbol of love is understandable in terms of a structure of comparison, the introduction of the Christ child is possible only through a narrative, a relation between a "first" and a "second" child, a life and a death that have already taken place. The temporal ordering of this narrative would attempt to contain the difference that cannot be systematized in conceptual structures. Like the narrative that appears in the metaphysical part of the system, this narrative exceeds the conceptual structure of the critical argument. But its emergence in the symbol indicates that the temporality of the narrative does not derive from an empirical model. The story that emerges at the joints of the system tells of the impossibility for the language of the system to close upon itself in its representation, a nonclosure that appears as the irrevocable "priority" of an event.

We might think of this nonclosure in terms of the difference between the symbol and its concept, or the symbol and its representation as an analogy. If the symbol represents the thinking of the relation of the sensible to the supersensible, the concept of the symbol—the definition of the symbol in critical discourse—enacts a kind of positing that cannot be recuperated symbolically. This nonrecuperation would be marked by the proliferation of examples, not "empirical" examples, but examples in the argument, linguistic examples, which would always eventually take the form of a narrative. The concept of the limit which structures the system would thus be made possible by the symbol and impossible by its concept. The articulation of parts of the system by the symbol would be made possible and impossible by the disarticulation of the symbol with itself. The limit, we might say then, is divided between the structure the symbol symbolizes and the story its example tells.[33]

We recognize this story, moreover, in the metaphysical example. If we reexamine the exemplary relation between transcendental philosophy and metaphysics in terms of the workings of the symbol, the narrative that emerges in the former— the death of matter for philosophy—appears to retell, or repeat, the symbolic sacrifice. Force, or the conceptualization of motion as continually falling, must be read not only in reference to a scientific calculation, but also in reference to the "fall" narrated in the symbol. But this latter reference is not a purely conceptual foundation of the example in the symbol, or the exemplary structure of empirical knowledge in limit-knowledge; for the "death" in this story is not part of a system of conceptualized relations. Rather, the "death" of matter, as the event of "force," re-marks the event in the self-symbolization of the system which founds and yet also exceeds its own knowledge. The engimatic externality of the event called "force," its exemplary position as an empirical example, marks an event that occurs, not in the empirical world, but "in" the system itself as language. The threat of the metaphysical example, that the conceptual system might be determined by something outside of it, is not therefore a threat that comes from the empirical world.[34] The externality upon which the system relies is to a certain extent, that is, only *figured* by the empirical world. The narrative that emerges in this figuration says very little indeed about the empirical world as such, and a good deal about the "externality" of the system to itself.[35]

The "remarkable' quality of the metaphysical example, in particular the example of inertia, thus lies in its double relation to physical science, on the one hand, and to the symbol on the other. While on the one hand the example of inertia exemplifies the articulation between the discursive science of philosophy and the laws of the empirical world, on the other hand it tells of a disarticulation of the discursive system with itself in the symbol. The relation between philosophy and empirical science is thus disrupted by the relation between the symbol and the example, a relation which would be akin to the relation between the different *linguistic* examples of the symbol in the text of the *Prolegomena* and its footnotes. The empirical example becomes, in this context, yet another linguistic example of a symbol. It tells less about the relation between discursive and nondiscursive knowledge than about the impossible relation of discursive knowledge to itself.

This double aspect of the exemplary-symbolic structure sheds some light on the split between "experience" and "empirical science" in Kant's system. For if "empirical science" refers to observation and mathematics, "experience" refers first of all to a philosophical vocabulary, the vocabulary of empirical philosophy (and in particular that of Hume). "Experience" is not a concept derived from empirical observation but a figure generated by discursive arguments to supplement their own self-representation. "Experience" thus functions as the linguistic example that always accompanies the empirical example. One could thus say that no matter how much it wants to, and indeed does refer to empirical law, a discursive text must also say "experience." And in saying that, it has left the empirical realm altogether and is telling the same old story of love and death, a story with neither a purely experiential nor purely spiritual meaning.

The impossibility of fully symbolizing itself thus turns philosophical criticism into something like a literary criticism. This is not a failure, indeed, but a form of rigor, the rigor that exhibits the necessity and impossibility of linking the laws of language to the laws of the empirical world, or of achieving systematic access to a "world" through language. To the extent that all discursive theory is subject to these necessities, the knowledge of theory will always fall into a similar pattern. What discursive theory knows will always be that it cannot know, entirely, what it is: and to this extent its object will always be "linguistic."[36] That is, in Kant's symbolic terms, there can be no *falling*, in theory, that is not also falling "*in love*." And the story of this love is not only a recollection of the world we know, but also a repetition of the event that divides us from it.[37]

4

SIGNS OF LOVE

"Remember me."

(Hamlet 1.5)

Sigmund Freud's writings on sexuality can be seen as a persistent attempt to understand the *error of experience* through its relation to a past. The mind's experience of itself in love, Freud suggests, is always in error; and it is sexuality which displays this error as the blindness, of love, to its own history. In his late work *Civilization and Its Discontents*, this critical perspective emerges in a new theoretical claim: that to be sexual, for civilized man, is to be guilty, or more specifically, that human consciousness, as a sexual consciousness, is ruled by an "unconscious sense of guilt." Through the concept of unconscious guilt, experience is, indeed, linked to a past, to a crime for which it is constantly atoning, the murder of a father. But what kind of crime is this, that can never be discovered in a memory, but only in a kind of forgetting, in an *unconscious* feeling? And what kind of past moreover is constituted by a crime that, as Freud will insist, is never committed by the individual but only by what he calls the primal horde of prehistory—a past, therefore, which never, for the individual, *occurs* as such?

These questions, in effect, are not simply about experience but about the way in which experience (in its error) comes to know itself, that is, about psychoanalytic inquiry and theory. In its peculiar juxtaposition of historical narratives, *Civilization* raises as many problems about the nature of its own mode of explanation as it does about the nature of its human subject. Critics have indeed attempted to account both for what it is exactly Freud is saying about love and for the problematic specificity of the very nature of the psychoanalytic mode.

When Lionel Trilling wrote of the literary power of *Civilization and Its Discontents*, he addressed these issues by insisting on the relation between the negative psychoanalytic knowledge of the psyche and what might be called the ethical stance of this knowledge, its capacity to "rescue an imperative."[1] The central thesis of *Civilization*, Trilling said, is that society, usually considered the cause of man's frustration, is no more than a "necessary" cause, and that "the direct cause of man's unhappiness is an element of the unconscious itself." This produces a disturbing knowledge of psychical inauthenticity:

> Must we not say that Freud's theory of the mind and of society has at its core a flagrant inauthenticity which it deplores but accepts as essential in the mental structure? Man's existence in civilization is represented as being decisively conditioned by a psychic entity which, under the mask of a concern with social peace and union, carries on a ceaseless aggression to no purpose save that of the enhancement of its own power, inflicts punishment for no act committed but only for a thought denied, and, so far from being appeased by acquiescence in its demands, actually increases its severity in the degree that it is obeyed.[2]

The negative insight of *Civilization* is the recognition that what appears to be an external conflict between man and society is in fact an internal conflict, a self-aggressivity and dissimulation which turns mental life into a "Tartuffian deceit practised by one part of the mind upon another."[3] But the purpose of this revelation is not knowledge. Asking why Freud ends his career on such a dark note, Trilling found the answer in the form this knowledge takes, the form of tragedy:

> From religion as it vanished Freud was intent upon rescuing one element, the imperative actuality which religion attributed to life . . . the momentous claim which life makes upon us . . . This [attitude shared with religion] we might call the tragic element of Judaism and Christianity, having reference to the actual literary genre of tragedy and its inexplicable power to activate, by the representation of suffering, a faith quite unrelated to hope . . . It is this authenticating imperative Freud wishes to preserve. He locates it in the dialectic of Eros and death, which is the beginning of man's nature.[4]

The negative knowledge of inauthenticity is transformed into the "rescuing" of an authenticating imperative by becoming tragedy. If the analogy with religion suggests an ethical dimension to this imperative (also present in the notion of "authentication"), this is because literature has been characterized here in the classical Kantian category of the aesthetic, which permits the passage between the realms of knowledge and of "freedom" or ethical action. While Trilling seems removed from the Kantian philosophical vocabulary, we can nonetheless recognize the concern he shares with Kant about the possibility for aesthetic form to link theory with the ethical realm. What is significant about the aesthetic function for Trilling is that the passage to the ethical is also the passage out of the enclosure of theoretical knowledge to life itself. This passage occurs, in Trilling's essay, through his notion of literary representation, which makes possible a kind of exchange between the discourse of theory and its human object: because the theory, as literary "representation," has "power," its object, "life" or "man's nature," issues an "imperative."[5] What *Civilization* thus achieves in the literary form of its theoretical knowledge is the attainment of an ethical stance issuing, not from theoretical reflection, but from life. As literature, this late psychoanalytic text turns theoretical understanding into the living experience of an ethical imperative. This imperative Trilling identified in Freud's text as "the dialectic of Eros and death."

If the literariness of *Civilization* consists, for Trilling, in how it makes possible a passage out of the theoretical realm, it consists for a number of readers within the structuralist tradition in the impossibility of transcending the structures of knowledge. Briefly stated, the structuralist innovation is to study theory as a linguistic construct. Specifically, this construct is examined in terms of the relation between the referential dimension of language and the signifying structures that make such reference possible. This focus has shifted attention from the movement between knowledge and ethical action to the problems that arise *within* the realm of knowledge. The possibility that reference to a nonlinguistic "object" may be based, not on an empirical reality, but on the self-signifying structures of language, suggests that all theoretical knowledge may ultimately always be knowledge *of* knowledge, rather than of what that knowledge supposedly refers to (life, man, the psyche, etc.). Structuralist readings of Freud focus on this tension between the illusion of reference and the impossibility of escaping "structure," which is manifested in the narrative form of his writings, especially the case histories and the late work on civilization and religion.[6] The literariness of Freud tells us the truth of an impossibility, the impossibility precisely of passing beyond signifying structures to a nonlinguistic reality.

Leo Bersani modifies this line of reasoning in one of the most striking and suggestive interpretations of the literary Freud, which discovers in the self-signifying dimension of Freud's writing a knowledge of theoretical failure. Bersani's discussion of *Civilization* suggests that Freud's work finally refers us back to its own argument, insofar as it fails as theory: "I wish to argue that the subject of [*Civilization*] is less the explicitly proposed antagonism between instinct and civilization than the moves by which that very argument is undone."[7] This self-referential movement in *Civilization* occurs, according to Bersani, through a breakdown of the dualisms upon which the theory is built. This breakdown occurs specifically in the relation between the terms *love* and *aggressiveness:* the fact that, as objects of the theory, they are ultimately equated means that what they tell of first is something about the "textuality" of the theory. In the elimination of the distinction between opposed terms, and the resulting "tautology" of their definitions, the theory circles back upon itself, revealing ultimately the impossibility for a theoretical discourse to ground its own basic concepts:

> We don't move *from* love *to* aggressiveness in *Civilization and Its Discontents;* rather, love is redefined, re-presented, *as* aggressiveness . . . civilization itself repeats, rather than opposes, the other two terms and thereby transforms the argument of Freud's work into a triple tautology: Sexuality = aggression = civilization. Furthermore, we should be alerted to the book's dualisms and linear arguments by its extremely curious system of circular and paradoxical definitions . . . To the extent that the explanatory logic of *Civilization and Its Discontents* is both tautological and circular, it is a rigorously psychoanalytic logic which mocks all the philosophically narrativizing procedures and distinctions of Freud the prophetic thinker. It breaks down the boundaries separating concepts, and thereby nicely exemplifies what might be called an oceanic textuality.[8]

For Bersani, the breakdown of the distinction between the theory's referents, love and aggressiveness, signifies the "oceanic" nature of the textuality of the theory: that love is aggressiveness means that theory is oceanic.[9] Since "oceanic" is taken from Freud's essay as a term that seems to indicate love but in fact hides aggression, Bersani is suggesting that the dissimulating relationship between love and aggression revealed *by* Freud's theory ultimately signifies the dissimulating nature of the theoretical knowledge *of* love and aggression. This self-circulation Bersani identifies in Freud's text in the term *aggression.*

It would seem that this sort of careful attention to the language of Freud's argument leaves little room for the ethical questions raised by Trilling; the impossibility of escaping the structures (or structural failures) of the discursive production of knowledge appears to foreclose any passage out of the epistemological abyss. Yet it is interesting to note that the final focus of Trilling on the dualism of "Eros and death" (as life's imperative) and the final focus of Bersani on the monism of "aggression" (as the self-signifying disruption of the text) places the difference between them *within* the argument of *Civilization* itself. For the two stories of the origin of conscience by which Freud explains civilization in chapter 7—in the individual, the child's denial of an aggressive impulse toward the parent, in the race, the actual murder of the father followed by a resurgence of love for him—are distinguished precisely by the monism of the first (in the beginning there are aggressive impulses) and the dualism of the second (in the beginning there is aggression *and* love). It would thus not seem to be the case that a conscious, philosophizing dualism of the theory is replaced by an unconscious, textual monism, for Freud's insistence on maintaining both stories in his theory is not an insistence on dualism but on *both* monism *and* dualism. This essay will suggest that *Civilization* may be exploring a more complex relation between the referential function of its language and the necessity of an imperative stance than the simple division between the realms of "knowledge" and "ethical action" would imply.

This more complex relation seems to be precisely the object of Jacques Lacan's inquiry. In *The Ethics of Psychoanalysis* Lacan suggests that the truth of *Civilization* derives from Freud's reading of the ethical imperative "Love thy neighbor as thyself."[10] This truth is characterized by Lacan neither as something psychoanalysis knows nor as an imperative it gives, but rather as something it "witnesses"—*witness* being a legal term which suggests both knowing and ethical action. Indeed, when Freud himself explicitly raises questions about the nature of his theory in *Civilization*, he stages them in terms of a dilemma perfect for a courtroom drama: the possibility of bearing witness to the scene of a murder. And the dilemma arises, moreover, precisely around the question of the two origins of conscience, of the choice between a monistic and a dualistic theory. We must therefore try to understand how the question of theory arises in Freud's argument in order to ask again what it is that *Civilization*, as neither simply philosophy nor religion, witnesses.

The Father

The central project of *Civilization*, as Trilling emphasizes, is to understand man's unhappiness in civilized society. More specifically, one could say that *Civilization* attempts to understand man insofar as he is *defined by* a conflictual relation to something outside of himself, which he calls "civilization." This conflict takes the form of a paradox: while civilization is the goal and glory of man's efforts, it is equally the source of his sexual frustration and unhappiness. As both a civilized and a sexual being, then, man exists in a perpetual double bind: he can fulfill one side of his nature only at the cost of the other. *Civilization* attempts to discover the basis of this conflict.

The fundamental insight of Freud's argument is that the conflictual relation between man and an external "civilization" is a mask or displacement of a conflict of man with himself, a conflict between sexuality and the "superego." This conflict operates in the individual in the unconscious "sense of guilt." The only way to understand this unconscious conflict, Freud suggests, is in terms of its origins in a past event in the individual's life. *Civilization* thus attempts to understand the predicament of the self, as a sexually self-prohibiting agent, in terms of the origins of the sense of guilt.

The theoretical problem that arises in *Civilization* concerns the nature of this origin. In chapter 7, Freud seems to have difficulty settling on a single origin for the sense of guilt, a dissatisfaction that appears to concern the place of the father. First, Freud suggests that guilt originates in the child's identification with an aggressive "authority." He rapidly rejects this, however, for the conclusion that guilt originates in the *child's* aggressive impulse and its denial, a dynamic independent of any actual father's role. But then, as if concerned about thus exiling the real father from the individual's life, Freud rediscovers him—being murdered by the primal horde. Suddenly Freud is faced with an accusing reader looming up before him:

> At this point I should not be surprised if the reader were to complain angrily, '. . . Either it is not true [*falsch*] that the sense of guilt [*das Schuldgefühl*] comes from suppressed aggressiveness, or else the whole story of the killing of the father is a fiction [*ein Roman*], and the children of primaeval man did not kill their fathers any more often than children do nowadays. Besides, if it is not fiction but a plausible piece of history [*Historie*], it would be a case of something happening which everyone expects to happen—namely, of a person feeling guilty [*dass man sich schuldig fühlt*] because he really has done something which cannot be justified. And of this event, which is after all an everyday occurrence, psycho-analysis has not yet given any explanation [*ist uns die Psychoanalyse die Erklärung schuldig geblieben*]."[11]

The "reader" first of all objects to the positing of two different and mutually exclusive origins: a wished-for act with no real parent, and a real act with a real parent. Essentially, the difference appears to be between an origin in a fiction (the wish to act) and in an event (the action). The addition of the primal father story thus makes the theory suggest both a real and a fictional origin at once. In not deciding between the two, the theory becomes itself a kind of fiction: either "false" or "a novel." And as a fiction, it can no longer provide any sort of reliable theoretical knowledge.

This objection raised explicitly by the reader would appear to be complicated, however, by the wording of the reader's accusation. In the German phrase used to make the final point, *die Pschoanalyse [ist uns] die Erklärung schuldig geblieben*—literally, "Psychoanalysis owes us an explanation"—the word for indebtedness, *schuldig,* is also the word used earlier in the paragraph to mean "guilty."[12] The problem *of* guilt is also the guilt of the theory: if the murder of the primal father is the cause of a problem in the psyche, the *concept* of this murder is the effect of a problem in the theory. The figure of the murdered father is thus the locus of a convergence between the originating *act* and the *knowledge* of that origination, between guilt and theory.[13]

This interplay of theory and its object, centered on the reality or fictionality of an originating event, would seem to raise the kind of issues emphasized by structuralist readings of the "primal scene" and "primal scene fantasy" in the Wolf-Man case. In these readings the central theoretical problem is whether the origin posited by the narrative is a real event, a primal scene, or a primal fantasy, determined by psychical structures. The structuralist decision for the latter implies that *what* the theory discovers at the origin is nothing other than the necessity of narrative structure itself, that is, that the structures of the psyche and of the theory are ultimately reflections of each other. Similarly, the problem of deciding, in *Civilization,* between an origin in an aggressive impulse (without a real father as object), and an origin in an aggressive act (against a real father), would appear to reiterate essentially the choice between structure and event. The insistence on both stories at once would suggest that the event, the murder of the father, is always in some sense fictional, because the event to which the theory refers is always ultimately a reflection of its own signifying structure. The guilt of theory would thus be precisely the effectiveness of the theory of guilt: for *Historie,* here, would be itself a function of *Roman.*

The reader's second objection, however, raises some problems. Even if the primal murder story is true, the reader says, it does not serve as an *explanation* of the sense of guilt. In this objection, the problem with the primal murder has nothing to do with fact or fiction, but with the possibility that, as an originating event, it may not be *understood* at all. Or rather it is an *event* that is not an *origin,* that does not allow for the creation of a narrative sequence and hence an understanding of the relation between the event and the conflict. This raises the possibility, likewise, that the "guilt" of the theory might not simply derive from the fact that the event, to which the theory refers, reflects its structure, but that the structure itself involves an "event" which cannot be made the object of a reflection. That is, the conflict created by the addition of the primal father story, or the "guilt" of referring to an action, might be connected with the way the theory "acts" in referring.

This other conflict introduces an asymmetry into the relation between object and theory, which can no longer be understood in terms of a symmetrical opposition between event and structure or reference and signification. This asymmetry seems to be reflected in the original set of alternatives posed by the reader: Either it is not true (*falsch*) that the sense of guilt comes from aggressiveness, or else the whole story of the killing of the father is a novel (*ein Roman*—not, as the translation says, "fiction," which returns it to a question of truth and falsehood). The alternative is not between truth and falsehood, but between truth and falsehood on the one hand, and literature on the other. The theory is guilty not because it is false or fictional, but because it won't decide between falsehood, a function of reference, and literature, something that can't be reduced to problems of truth and falsehood, and appears to involve some sort of action as well. The relation between the guilty subject and the guilty theory cannot therefore be understood in terms of action or event and knowledge or structure, but rather in terms of the way in which knowing is acting, or reference to an event is itself traversed by an occurrence. In order to understand this guilt we must return to the origin, as it were, of the argument, to the scene of a reading. Here we will encounter, not a father, but an equally threatening character, the neighbor.

The Neighbor

Freud begins the analysis of unhappy man in chapter 5. Civilization, he has pointed out, creates an unbearable conflict for the sexual self. For while living with others in a civilized manner produces many benefits for the individual, it demands, as a price, the investment of the same libidinal energy that goes into his sexual relationships. To live sexually and to live in society are in some sense mutually exclusive, since each demands the energy needed for the other. The paradigm for this conflict Freud discovers in the encounter of man with a commandment, "Love thy neighbor as thyself." It is the neighbor's imperative presence, the command to give him love, which drains the individual of his libidinal energy. Freud's analysis will attempt to understand the necessity of the neighbor, this third party who drops in uninvited on sexual exchanges. Psychoanalytic theory will be a matter of putting the neighbor in his place.

The argument proceeds through a kind of dramatization, which puts on the stage an irritable and parsimonious self, personally resentful of the ethical command it encounters. The conflict between man and civilization is thus dramatized in the struggle between the speaker in the passage and the command. The speaker appears as a narcissistic ego, faced with a neighbor who invades his loving self-relation:

> Let us adopt a naive attitude towards [the command], as though we were hearing it for the first time; we shall be unable then to suppress a feeling of surprise and bewilderment. Why should we do it? What good will it do us? But, above all, how shall we achieve it? How can it be possible? My love is something which I ought not to throw away without reflection . . . If I love someone, he must deserve it in some way . . . But if I am to love him (with this universal love) merely because he, too, is an inhabitant of this earth, like an insect, an earth-worm or a grass-snake, then I fear that only a small modicum of my love will fall to his share—not by any possibility as much as, by the judgment of my reason, I am entitled to retain for myself. What is the point of a precept enunciated with so much solemnity if its fulfilment cannot be recommended as reasonable? (109–10)

The neighbor enters here as an annoying disruption of a narcissistic specular relation of the self to itself.[14] Significantly, however, the neighbor is not introduced directly but by way of

a text, a verbal imperative: the encounter is thus characterized
not as the actual meeting of two human beings, but as a disruptive relation between the imperative to neighborly love and the
statement "I love myself." The "parsimoniousness" of the self
in this passage (Lacan's word for the economic argument of the
speaker) [15] suggests that in the latter statement, the *meaning* of
"love" depends entirely on the uniqueness of the referent "myself": love means a relation between two selves only insofar as
it always points back to this unique self-reference. To this extent "love" names, not a psychological relation between people
or within the self, but a verbal potential, the possibility of the
self referring to itself. The conflict between man and civilization around "love" is thus a conflict involved in the constitution of the self through specular self-reflection. It is a conflict
encountered by the self attempting to refer to itself, that is, to
say "I love myself."

This self-constituting character, who speaks the argument
to us, tells us first of all precisely how the command conflicts
with the concept of a unique self. The problem with the command, the argument makes clear, is not just the order to love
the neighbor, but to love the neighbor *as* the self. What is
wrong with this, the speaker implies, is that it assumes that, in
love, self and neighbor can be exchanged or substituted for
each other. That is, "I love myself" must always *also* mean, "I
love my neighbor (=anyone else)." [16] In this exchange the self is
not a unique referent, but a figure for the neighbor, and vice
versa. And if the self and the neighbor are just figures for each
other, then "self" and "neighbor" are no longer anchored, as
referents, in actual objects in the world, but rather depend entirely on a signifying act, that is, they are fictions created *by*
"love." Love, in this case, always refers back to itself; it is no
longer aimed at any object in the world but only at the act of
loving. To love is to love love, and all apparent referents become ultimately figures for this self-signifying structure. What
the command leads to, the argument thus implies, is a purely
figurative understanding of the self. The speaker objects to

what could be considered a kind of structuralism implicit in the command, which establishes an equality between the self and the other only by transforming their differences into the artificiality of a symmetrical system of figurative exchanges, or the emptiness of a signifying structure. The self is literally lost in "love."

As the argument continues, the command's universalizing of love is shown to be not only in conflict with the idea of a unique self, but based upon an error. This error is demonstrated through the phenomenon of hatred or aggression. Hatred reveals, in the relation between self and neighbor, the operation of another principle than that of symmetrical exchange:

> On closer inspection, I find still further difficulties. Not merely is this stranger in general unworthy of my love; I must honestly confess that he has more claim to my hostility and even my hatred . . . If it will do him any good he has no hesitation in injuring me . . . Indeed, he need not even obtain an advantage; if he can satisfy any sort of desire by it, he thinks nothing of jeering at me, insulting me, slandering me and showing his superior power; and the more secure he feels and the more helpless I am, the more certainly I can expect him to behave like this to me. . . .
>
> Now it is very probable that my neighbor, when he is enjoined to love me as himself, will answer exactly as I have done and will repel me for the same reasons. . . .
>
> The element of truth behind this . . . is that . . . their neighbor is for [men] not only a potential helper or sexual object, but also someone who tempts them to satisfy their aggressiveness on him, to exploit his capacity for work without compensation, to use him sexually without his consent, to seize his possessions, to humiliate him, to cause him pain, to torture and to kill him. (111)

"Hatred" here is defined purely in terms of its structural relation to "love." It is, specifically, a kind of reversal of the principle of exchange which characterized the absolute generality of love (as the substitutability of self and neighbor): if there is any exchange between me and my neighbor, these passages imply, it is only insofar as we hate (i.e., aggress) each other. In this reversal, the figurative elimination of differences in "love" is literalized as the actual annihilation of the other's body: we get rid of the other's difference not through their figurative similarity to us but through their actual removal. By showing its structural relation to love, this literalized understanding of difference is shown to be paradoxically implicit in the command's assumption that all people can be equally figures for each other. This assumption, we now see, itself depends upon a figure that is taken literally, the figure of difference as symmetrical relaton. The "structuralism" of brotherly love subordinates difference (implied in the verb "to love") to a closed system of signifying exchanges without reflecting on the figure of this subordination. This moment of blindness or literalization necessarily returns, Freud implies, in the form of real aggression, the mistaking of the empirical existence of the other as a threat to the unity of the self. In ignoring this figurative dimension, or literalizing its own basic figure, the command eliminates the possibility of otherness, an elimination taking the form of violent oppression.

What does this symptom tell us about the self? Freud claims, as we recall, to be discovering in this chapter not just an *error* in civilization but the *necessity* of the conflict between civilization and the self. This necessity is not to be found on the level of explicit criticism, in the chapter, but on the level of its dramatization, in which a narcissistic self faces a repressive other in the commandment. The constitution of this narcissistic self, it turns out, depends on much the same structure as the constitution of neighborly love: it depends on a kind of recognition of itself, *as hating others,* in the command, an exchange between itself and the commandment as "hatred." "Hatred toward others" becomes the figure that joins self and commandment—that allows the persona to recognize in the commandment an expression of its own narcissistic self—just as "love" was the figure that was to join self and neighbor, to make the self recognize itself as the same as the neighbor. In this self-recognition in hatred, the self is constituted, as was neighborly love, by a nonrecognition of otherness, in this case the otherness of the commandment itself (we could say: in order to read the neighbor as utterly different, the persona reads the commandment as a figure of the same, hence repeating the commandment's original error). The appearance of the (aggressive) commandment over against the self in the chapter can thus be analyzed in similar fashion to the analysis of the neighbor and self in the commandment: instead of representing the same—the unity of the self in its hatred of others—it represents a difference, the disunity of the self in its aggression against itself. That is, the commandment is precisely the place in which the "neighbor" turns against the self, not as the "same" self, nor as entirely different from the self, but rather as the otherness of the self to itself. If the "truth" of the commandment is hatred toward others, its particular appearance (as a command to love) is a form of the self's aggression toward itself.

This analysis introduces a far-reaching reversal of perspectives which resembles, but is more radical than, the reversal between neighborly love and hatred. While we started with a conflictual relation between *love* of self and of neighbor, the hidden "truth" of which was "hatred," we are now faced with *hatred* of self and of neighbor. This relation could also be considered conflictual insofar as the action of the command (against the self) belies the meaning of the command: just as the claim of the command (to love) denies (even while it acts out) aggression toward the neighbor, the claim of the analysis (to hate) could be said to deny (even while it acts out) aggression toward the self. The deeper irony that runs through this chapter tells us it is not "hatred" but "love" which is the ultimate culprit, love which operates against the self's attempt to annihilate itself. In the dark vision of Freud's argument, the problem of civilization is not, ultimately, that in order to love ourselves we must aggress others, but that we aggress others because we have failed adequately to aggress, that is to eliminate, ourselves.[17]

This failure is represented in the chapter as a kind of asymmetry structured into the violence between the neighbor and the self. First of all, the certainty of "my" hatred toward the neighbor is answered only by a conjecture about the neighbor: Freud can only say that "it is probable" that my neighbor will respond to me as I to him—aggression may not indeed be reciprocal at all. Similarly, in the final paragraph on hatred, aggression is not represented merely as war—that is, as the symmetrical, negative version of a loving exchange—but as something more akin to *revenge*.[18] Revenge is not the reversal of a loving exchange but an ever-escalating, never-completed violence that cannot stop, because each act that eliminates a person produces another to be eliminated. The excesses of revenge tragedies indeed always occur as the failure to exchange one violent act for another, to end violence by violence: the attempt to end all violence becomes instead its endless *repetition*. Revenge can thus be seen here as a never-completed task which reestablishes the self at the very moment of its destruction. Aggression is never quite the self's undoing, but only the threat (or promise) of it: hatred emerges as aggression, not against the self, but against the neighbor, and it is only through the neighbor that I may be destroyed, never at my own will. From this point of view, the battle between self and neighbor is the endless failure of the self's battle against itself.

Chapter 5 thus shows the entire conflict between self and civilization in "love" to be a kind of displacement of a deeper conflict between that entire arena of meaning and, on the other hand, nonmeaning (the elimination of the self). The errors that define the conflict between self-reference and figuration, expressed in the literalizing form of hatred or aggression, reflect what might be called the error of meaning itself, the fact that the very establishment of meaning (in the appearance of "love") is itself, somehow, an error. It is the possibility of the success, rather than the failure of reference, that becomes the original mistake. This originating error of meaning is represented in revenge as a kind of temporal lapse within meaning.

Revenge, as an endless succession of violent acts, is defined as a response to an action in the past, as the repetition of a *past* aggression. Thus, if aggression means, in this chapter, that the self can't lose itself in hatred—if it means that we simply can't get rid of ourselves—this means also that we can't *forget* ourselves, which is a specifically temporal dilemma.[19] The self arises in conflict with time: if it is from the beginning too *early* to love, it is already too *late* to die. Thus, when the neighbor confronts the self in chapter 5, it confronts it not as a mirror-image, nor as a present aggressor, but rather as the figure of another that returns from the past, a ghost that can never quite be encountered. This conflict marks the "origin" of the conflicted self in the failure *not to mean,* a failure repeated endlessly in aggression toward the other.

Chapter 7 will attempt to discover the scene of this origination, to locate the origin of the ghost, or the crime in which the self is created in this conflict. Psychoanalysis, here, essentially tries to put the neighbor in his place by finding his place in the past. The movement from chapter 5 to chapter 7 can thus be seen as the attempt of theory to put an end, as it were, to the endless repetition of the violence by exchanging it for understanding, the understanding of the "origin." In this movement psychoanalysis itself appears to stand under a kind of imperative: the knowledge of the disruption in meaning must, it seems, become narrative, the history of the divided self. Narrative is a must: the language of the theory, in articulating the truth of the language of the self, neither simply refers nor figures, but narrates. If the self is placed under an imperative to "love," we could say, the theory reads this imperative as a command to remember—to remember the figure of the father. It is in this movement of the theory in chapter 7 that we can thus learn about the error of the self that appears in chapter 5. What the chapter bears witness to is not only to be found, therefore, in what it says about the encounter it discovers at the origin of the conflicted self, but also in what it does in the remembering of this encounter, in the encounter of its remembering.

Fathers and Sons

> "The spirit I have seen may be a devil."
> (*Hamlet* 2.2)

Chapter 7 begins, then, not with the conflict between self and neighbor, but with a temporal predicament in the self: the conflict between the instinctual side of the self and the super ego, which speaks its prohibitions in a voice *from the past*. This haunted struggle takes the form of the "sense of guilt," which prevents the self from fulfilling its desires. In attempting to trace the origin of this feeling in a past event, the argument attempts to understand, essentially, the paradoxical origin of meaning as error. It attempts to give meaning, that is, to the origin of meaning. Thus the theory plays out many of the patterns enacted by the self in chapter 5, in the form of the search for an origin: if the self discovered its own meaning in the commandment, the theory recognizes *itself* as meaningful, we could say, in the concept of the origin. Thus the theory will also attempt to discover a relation between meaning and the world, that is, to understand the division in the self in terms of its referential connection, or figurative lack of connection, with empirical reality. This connection at the origin is represented, here, as the encounter between father and son. Whereas the "neighbor" was, in chapter 5, the locus of a kind of insight and blindness in the self's definition of itself, the "father" becomes, in this chapter, the place in which the theory faces its own knowledge and blindness in relation to the "self" that it analyzes.

It is not surprising, then, that the analysis shows a certain similarity to the analysis in chapter 5. Freud begins with an illusory narrative of origins, which is then replaced by a more truthful account which reverses the first. After arriving at this truth, however, he suddenly introduces a third story to supplement the second one, which in many ways resembles the original one he rejected. It is in this movement that the interest of the chapter lies, for it follows the law already laid out in the reading of the ethical imperative. The movement from a simple model of reference, to a model of figuration, to a supplement that appears much like the original referential model is itself a kind of narrative which tells a story, not about the self but about theory. It is the story of a theoretical language attempting to tell the whole truth about language. It is in reading this story of theory that we can also attempt to understand some of the problems raised around the self.

The first narrative traces the split between ego and super-ego to a relation between child and external authority. The basis of the figuration in which the superego speaks from within the self is represented as an act of identification with the authority and internalization of the external division:

> First comes renunciation of instinct owing to fear of aggression by the *external* authority (this is, of course, what fear of loss of love amounts to, for love is a protection against this punitive aggression). After that comes the erection of an *internal* authority [*Aufrichtung der inneren Autorität*], and renunciation of instinct owing to fear of it—owing to fear of conscience. In this second situation bad intentions are equated with bad actions, and hence come a sense of guilt and a need for punishment. The aggressiveness of conscience keeps up the aggressiveness of the authority. (128)

> A threatened external unhappiness—loss of love and punishment on the part of the external authority—has been exchanged for a permanent internal unhappiness, for the tension of the sense of guilt. (128)

This story models the division in the self on a real empirical relation in the world. The father, here, is originally a perceived object which is internalized through or identified with in an exchange of the properties of internal and external worlds, of external loss and internal gain: the father is maintained as a loving object by turning the aggressive or lost father into an internal faculty. This sets up, within the psyche, an ego-superego relation based on an economy of sacrificial exchange: spiritual pleasure for libidinal renunciation. This model of the psyche resembles the classical Aristotelian model of metaphor as an analogy with and transcendence of the perceptual world (literal exchanged for figurative, empirical reality exchanged for fictional, etc.). The originating impulse of the figuration is understood as an external loss or absence (loss of the father's love), that is, a threat imposed from without. It is this loss which is reiterated and becomes the principle of the division between ego and superego. The narrative thus models the aggressivity of the self, or the split between ego and superego, on an empirical fact (real act of aggression as loss of the object of love). The origin of the conflict between love and hatred, or the meaning of the conflicted figurations of the self, is essentially based on a referential relation to the world.

Freud explains the insufficiency of this model by pointing out that the ego-superego relation does not in fact operate on an economy of exchange. Recalling his comments on the neighbor who becomes more aggressive as the self becomes more helpless, Freud points out that "it is precisely the people who have carried saintliness the farthest who reproach themselves with the worst sinfulness," and that for them, "virtue forfeits some of its promised reward" (126). The alternative narrative reverses the model of analogical relation:

> Conscience (or more correctly, the anxiety which later becomes conscience) is indeed the cause of instinctual renunciation to begin with, but . . . later the relationship is reversed [*kehrt sich das Verhältnis um*]. Every renunciation of instinct now becomes a dynamic source of conscience and every fresh renunciation increases the latter's severity and intolerance. If we could only bring it into harmony with what we already know about the history of the origin of conscience, we should be tempted to defend the paradoxical statement that conscience is the result of instinctual renunciation, or that instinctual renunciation (imposed on us from without) creates conscience, which then demands further renunciation. (128–29)

The "reversal" (*Umkehrung*)[20] of agent and instinctual renunciation has the effect of placing at the origin not a relation of perception and identification, that is, of analogy or metaphor, but an act. The act is, moreover, not an empirical one in the world but an act of the mind upon itself: the "denial" (*Verzicht*) of an impulse. If we understand the impulse as an impulse aimed at the world, then the relation to the superego begins here as the denial of a referential relation to any object whatsoever (including itself).[21] Since Freud has earlier suggested that we think of this impulse as an aggressive one, the impulse and its denial create the aggressive relation of commandment and self of chapter 5, in which the commandment is essentially a form of aggression against the self. The dynamic of self-aggression and aggression toward the other, or the conflictual relation of the self and society, is grounded in an independent act of figuration, in the primacy of figure over reference.[22]

In the rejection of the first for the second story of origins, then, the theory to some extent provides a kind of structuralist revision of empirical theories of the mind. How then are we to understand the third narrative, the story of the primal father, which Freud claims must supplement the story of the individual? Freud gives us one hint in his suggestion, discussed above, that in introducing this narrative the theory becomes "guilty": if the "guilt" of the individual is characterized by the speaking of the imperative, then the guilt of the theory may be its own subjection to an imperative as well. In this imperative, the father returns as a referent in the world, but not exactly as an empirical one, since he returns in his death. That is, the third story does not simply reintroduce a reference based on an analogy with perceptual objects, but rather a reference based on, precisely, the representation of death. With the primal father it is not so much the empirical world, but the dead, that returns as an empirical referent:

> It can also be asserted that when a child reacts to his first great instinctual frustrations with excessively strong aggressiveness and with a correspondingly severe super-ego, he is following a phylogenetic model and is going beyond the response that would be currently justified; for the father of prehistoric times was undoubtedly terrible, and an extreme amount of aggres-

siveness may be attributed to him . . . Man's sense of guilt . . .
was acquired at the killing of the father by the brothers banded
together. . . .

    Where, in this case, did the remorse come from? . . . This re-
morse was the result of the primordial ambivalence of feeling
towards the father. His sons hated him, but they loved him,
too. After their hatred had been satisfied by their act of aggression, their love came to the fore in their remorse for the deed. It
set up [*richtete* . . . *auf*] the super-ego by identification with the
father . . . Now, I think, we can at last grasp two things perfectly clearly: the part played by love in the origin of conscience
and the fatal inevitability of the sense of guilt . . . The sense of
guilt is an expression of the conflict due to ambivalence, of the
eternal struggle between Eros and the instinct of destruction or
death . . . So long as the community assumes no other form
from that of the family, the conflict is bound to express itself in
the Oedipus complex, to establish the conscience and to create
the first sense of guilt. (131–32)

The father enters here, essentially, as the object *of* his murder.
He is known by his sons, but is known essentially as dead: this
is expressed, in the narrative, by the fact that the sons experience their love for him only after he has died. He is thus an
object of reference only retrospectively, as already dead, and
hence is not properly an object of perception. Similarly, the
specular self-recognition of the sons in the dead father, as his
"murderer," is a retrospective reconstruction of the cause of his
death. The narrative thus reintroduces reference not around a
perceptual world, but around death. It is a relation *to death*
which now grounds the figure of the father in something other
than "mere" figure. The primal father story thus appears to
represent, in some way, the unrecognized *action* that took place
in the theorization of the second story (much as the truth of
the commandment, hatred, revealed the unrecognized suppression of difference involved in its figure of love).

    The link between the second and third stories would ap-
pear to be, specifically, the way in which the father is *not there*
at the origin: in the story of the individual, the father is absent;
in the story of the race, he is dead. (We might say that if the sec-

ond story represents death as absence, the third story attempts to understand the error of that representation.) In the second story, this absence of the father, or absence of an empirical basis of figuration, permitted the autonomy of figuration which was opposed to reference. In the third story, it is precisely death which ties the "father" figure, once again, to something other than itself, which subjects the superego's autonomy to a law, but a law that is not that of the empirical world. The very possibility of conceiving of figuration as autonomous in the second story depends, it would seem, on a relation that is not, itself, autonomous, although it is also not subject to empirical law. It is this relation which appears to necessitate, and is represented in, the telling of the third story. If the second story, the origin of the superego in the aggression toward an absent father, is the triumph of a psychoanalytic theory (of figure), the third story tells us something about the conditions of this (figure of) theory.

The appearance of the third story would thus seem, at this point, to provide a critique of structuralism similar to the one made of the commandment in chapter 5. The literal elimination of the father in the second story, the third story would seem to tell us, is a kind of literalization which marks a moment of blindness in the definition of the origin as an autonomous act of figuration. Freud's insistence on maintaining *both* stories would be akin to the persona's insistence, in chapter 5, that the commandment to love manifests hatred. The theory of the individual—the autonomy of aggression—is necessary (like the commandment), but by itself is in error; the whole truth can be understood only through the addition of the primal father story. The relation between the role of the father in both stories—as absent and as dead—thus defines a kind of closure for psychoanalysis as a completely self-critical theory of the self as well as of theory.

The death of the father does not, however, entirely define the position of the third story. For the presence of the father in this story is not directly the memory of a dead man, but the

remorseful memory of the *murder*. It is not just the death but
the murder which sets going the memory of, or reference to,
the father, by spurring the feeling of "love." The event speaks,
as the imperative to remember, through love, a fact represented
by the association of the story with the Oedipus Complex and
hence with the Oedipal mother, who is an object of love only
insofar as she is a taboo spoken by the dead father. If the aggressive father of the first (referential) story returns, in the
third story, in his death, the love of the father in the first story
returns, in the third story, with a different face, not just the face
of the father but of the Oedipal mother. The appearance of the
mother by the side of the dead father is the sign of the law by
which the individual story must give rise to the primal history,
but a sign which remains, in this movement, unread.

The mother, then, marks the connection between the story
of the individual and that of the race. The importance of the
mother as the link between these stories is represented by the
fact that the Oedipal conflict is said to be the effect of "primal
ambivalence" (what operated in the race) in the life of the individual. The mother thus represents the necessity that ties the
theory of the individual to the story of primal history, a necessity that remains unconscious, unread, in the theorization of
the father. If the ethical imperative, then—the law of the guilty
self—speaks from its origins in the father, it is in the place of
the mother that we must seek the law that governs the "guilty"
theory, the law of the law.

But what kind of a place is this, and how can one speak
from it? If the Oedipal mother is the place, she is not the voice
of this other law. How then are we to understand this other
imperative? And who speaks it?

The Mother

The Oedipal mother has no voice in this passage; she is only
seen as a figure of love, a locus for the speech of the father. But

she is not the only mother around. In reintroducing the father in the primal father story, Freud also reintroduces a term, used in the first rejected story of the internalized father, that has curious female resonances in his text. The term is *aufrichten*, to set up or establish, used in both narratives to designate the institution of the superego (*Aufrichtung der inneren Autorität*—"establishment of an inner authority"; "*richtete . . . das Über-Ich auf*"—"established . . . the super-ego"). Earlier in *Civilization* Freud uses this word to designate the origin of sexual conflict in an alternative hypothesis about civilization which remains, however, confined to several footnotes. This hypothesis, mentioned at the end of chapter 4, attempts to locate sexual conflict, not in an opposition between civilization and sexuality (or ultimately in the struggle between Eros and Thanatos), but in sexuality itself. In the appended footnote Freud offers several theses in support of his suggestion (the phenomena of bisexuality and of sadistic sexuality)[23] and then turns eagerly to a third:

> The conjecture which goes deepest, however, is the one which takes its start from what I have said above in my footnote . . . It is to the effect that, with the assumption of an erect posture by man [*mit der Aufrichtung des Menschen*] and with the depreciation of his sense of smell, it was not only his anal erotism which threatened to fall a victim to organic repression, but the whole of his sexuality; so that since this, the sexual function has been accompanied by a repugnance which cannot further be accounted for, and which prevents its complete satisfaction and forces it away from the sexual aim into sublimation and libidinal displacements. (106, n.3)

At the origin of sexual unfulfillment, of the permanent inadequacy of the sexual object, is a simple movement: man stands up. This standing-up (*Aufrichtung*) corresponds precisely to the moment, in the primal father story, of the setting-up (*Aufrichtung*)[24] of the superego in primal man: it is the origin of sexual conflict. The origin "within" Eros figures the beginning not as an act of complete elimination (as murder) but as an exclusion, a movement *away from* something repugnant, a smell.

In the earlier footnote referred to in the note in chapter 4, we discover the gender of this smell:

> [The] change [in the affect of the organic periodicity of the sexual process on psychical sexual excitation] seems most likely connected with the diminution of the olfactory stimuli by means of which the menstrual process produced an effect on the male psyche. Their role was taken over by visual excitations which, in contrast to the intermittent olfactory stimuli, were able to maintain a permanent effect. The taboo on menstruation is derived from this 'organic repression', as a defence against a phase of development that has been surmounted . . . The diminution of the olfactory stimuli seems itself to be a consequence of man's raising himself from the ground, of his assumption of an upright gait [*Folge der Abwendung des Menschen von der Erde, des Entschlusses zum aufrechten Gang*] . . . The fateful process of civilization would thus have set in with man's adoption of an erect posture [*die Aufrichtung des Menschen*]. (99, n.1)

In standing up, in "turning away from the earth," man turns, specifically, from the female genitals, from menstruation as the smell of the woman. And this standing-up of man on his own is the turn away from, in particular, the earth, mother earth, the smell of the mother. As in the primal father story, the taboo that marks the origin of civilization and of sexual conflict is a taboo against the mother, but in this case not the incest taboo against a love-object, but the "taboo on menstruation," a taboo which makes visual representation of an object possible in the first place.[25] The taboo on menstruation is thus the exclusion of the mother, which grounds and disrupts the fulfilling nature of the object of sexual desire. While she enters as an alternative theory in the footnotes, this pre-Oedipal mother's connection to the main theory by way of the word *aufrichten* should alert us to a closer link she may bear to the function of the Oedipal mother in this story. One might express this relation by saying that, if in the individual and phylogenetic stories Freud seems to have produced not quite enough father (he is either absent or dead), he has simultaneously introduced, in the latter story, a little too much mother. Or rather: reintroduced her. For a mother, a rejected mother, has figured in Freud's essay from the beginning, in his confrontation with Romain Rolland which sets *Civilization* going, in the critique in which Freud stands up to his theoretical opponent.

Civilization begins as a response to a letter written by Freud's friend in criticism of an earlier work, *The Future of an Illusion*. Rolland has argued that Freud's analysis of the origins of religious feeling in this piece are incomplete because they do not account for the "oceanic feeling," a sense of "eternity" and of "something limitless and unbounded." For Rolland, this is the origin of the need for religion. Freud responds, and thus begins *Civilization* with a typical tone of irony: having characterized Rolland as one of civilization's generous few, he adds that Rolland's argument causes him "no small difficulty" because, he says, "I cannot discover this 'oceanic' feeling in myself." Unoceanic as he is, he goes on to characterize the oceanic feeling in terms of "the consolation offered by an original and somewhat eccentric dramatist to his hero who is facing a self-inflicted death. 'We cannot fall out of this world.'" This most admirable man's idea of the origin of religion is, Freud lightly suggests, the rationalization of the self at the moment of its most violent self-aggression, suicide. Nonetheless, or rather precisely because it is so illusory, Freud will spend the rest of the chapter arguing against it.

The significance of Rolland's argument is clearly not its position as a viable alternative to the theory of religion, but as an error in need of a critique.[26] Indeed, Rolland holds the same position as the command in chapter 5 and the first theory of origins in chapter 7: it is a *text* from which the knowledge of psychoanalysis will be derived as an interpretation. The error is, if we follow Freud's suggestion, based on an illusion of the possibility of direct and unique reference. This is expressed through the characterization of Rolland's theory via the Grabbe quotation, in terms of the figure of *not falling*. It will be precisely the possibility of falling that underlies the operation of the superego. Thus, against Grabbe's *Ja, aus der Welt werden wir nicht fallen,* Freud will gleefully produce, in a footnote to chapter 5, Heine's neighborly *Ja, man muss seinen Feinden verzeihen, aber nicht früher, als sie gehenkt werden* ("Yes, one must forgive one's enemies, but not before they have been hanged" [110]). *Hanging* is the sort of falling—not off the earth, but toward it—that characterizes the effects of the superego upon the ego.

The truth of *Civilization* is thus represented as the truth of its analytic interpretation of Rolland's illusion. This illusion, moreover, is characterized by an error in gender. Rolland, Freud will admit, has indeed located an origin; it is just that it isn't the origin of religion. What he has located is an early stage of the ego and of an ego-feeling (one suspects a narcissistic ego-feeling) that may remain in some people. And this goes back to a specific relation to a particular parent:

> An infant at the breast does not as yet distinguish his ego from the external world as the source of the sensations flowing in upon him. . . .
>
> If we may assume that there are many people in whose mental life this primary ego feeling has persisted to a greater or lesser degree, it would exist in them side by side with the narrower and more sharply demarcated ego-feeling. (66–68)

The oceanic feeling goes back to the sense of unity with the mother, the pre-Oedipal, pre-objective mother. As a feeling, Freud accepts this, but insofar as it might be considered the origin of religion, Freud replies:

> To me the claim does not seem compelling. After all, a feeling can only be a source of energy if it is itself the expression of a strong need. The derivation of religious needs from the infant's helplessness and the longing for the father aroused by it seems to me incontrovertible . . . I cannot think of any need in childhood as strong as the need for a father's protection. Thus the part played by the oceanic feeling, which might seek something like the restoration of limitless narcissism, is ousted from a place in the foreground [*ist . . . vom Vordergrund abgedrängt*]. (72)

Not the mother but the father. Freud stands up to Rolland by turning away from the all-embracing mother's presence to the father's absence, from pre-objective unity to objectlessness as the origin of religion and civilization. He thus establishes a theory that will ultimately ground the ego-superego relation in loss and internalization. If the theory centers its reading on the civilized "illusion" of the imperative to neighborly love, it begins with an interpretation of the "illusion" of the pre-Oedipal mother. Indeed, the entrance of the neighbor in some sense depends on this reading of the mother, or, as Freud puts it, of "ousting" the mother "from the foreground."

Mothers, however, are no more easily eliminated than fathers. As we have seen, the mother returns often in *Civilization*, if only in the footnotes, not as an ego feeling but at the origins of conflict. But what is the meaning of this return of the "pre-objective" mother in the form of conflict (and in a footnote)? And what relation does she bear to the absent father? We may begin to look for an answer to this question in yet another footnote, not a footnote to an alternative theory but to a literary piece which is said to illustrate the main theory. This footnote, it turns out, is in a very significant place: it is appended to the sentence, in chapter 4, preceding the sentence that elicits the footnote on the woman's smell. Freud writes:

> The sexual life of civilized man is . . . severely impaired; it sometimes gives the impression of being in process of involution as a function, just as our teeth and hair seem to be as organs. One is probably justified in assuming that its importance as a source of feelings of happiness, and therefore in the fulfilment of our aim in life, has sensibly diminished.[2] (105)

The footnote reads:

> [2] Among the works of that sensitive English writer, John Galsworthy, who enjoys general recognition today, there is a short story of which I early formed a high opinion. It is called 'The Apple-Tree', and it brings home to us how the life of present-day civilized people leaves no room for the simple natural love of two human beings. (105)

Just before he turns to an alternative theory (the theory of the pre-objective mother in the next footnote), Freud will illustrate the main theory with literature. This footnote would seem an unnotable aside were it not for the fact that here, too, in the Galsworthy story, we will come across another mother. Again, the father of the main text, the dead father, discovers at his side, or at his feet—at the feet of the main text—a mother. But if the relation between text and footnote represents, in the case of the "smell" story, the relation between main theory and alternative theory—two different choices—it represents here the relation between "theory" and "story," between history and *Roman*. This relation, we recall, defined the problem of the two stories of the father in chapter 7, the story of the individual and the race, the two stories bound by the Oedipal mother. In the footnoting of the Galsworthy story, then, the question of the relation between these two stories is raised again, the question concerning the law that governs the theory itself. In citing the story, Freud asks, in different terms, the question of the angry reader of chapter 7. Is this history or a just a novel? But the answer will not be found, as it is in chapter 7, *within* the argument, but rather in the relation between argument and footnote. In order to understand the relation between the two stories, the law of theory, we must read the relation between theory and the literary example that is to illustrate it. In order to understand the question of the father, we must ask the question of literature. At the intersection of these questions, the mother, "ousted from her place in the foreground," comes back on stage.

The Stepmother

"The Apple Tree" is all about foregrounds and backgrounds. Its final lines, an exchange between husband and wife, center on the composition of a painting:

> "Is the foreground right, Frank?"
> "Yes."

"But there's something wanting, isn't there?"
Ashurst nodded. Wanting? The apple tree, the singing, and the gold! And he solemnly put his lips to her forehead. It was his silver-wedding day.[27]

The question about the painting is also, in the husband's response, an answer about desire: how the desire of a man for his wife, the "wanting" of the wife, is marred by an irretrievable loss, something "wanting" in her. It is Freud's answer in *Civilization*. But question and answer are posed through a dialogue around a painting, in which both the question and the silent answer—words taken from a translation of Euripides' *Hippolytus*—refer to works of art. The relation between man and woman, the posing of the question of desire, is mediated through their relation to art, to what they see and don't see in it, to the way in which it determines how they see or don't see themselves and each other. And this is also, at the same time, the question of theory, for when Ashurst answers the question, he answers by illustrating his idea with a story, by illustrating his concept of desire with literature. To this extent the story tells not only the theory of *Civilization* but its own place in the theory.

The central act of seeing which structures the story is not, however, of a painting, but of a grave, a grave at a crossroads. Or rather a "mound of earth," "by the side of the road," which the wife points out to her husband as the story opens. When the story closes, the husband has "retraced his steps to the crossroads" to listen to a lame man telling the story of a death. A crossroads, a lame man and a death: one isn't surprised that this story was chosen as an illustration! On their silver-anniversary day, Frank and Stella Ashurst have stopped for lunch on their visit to the place where they first met. At this stop, it is the wife who first spots the mound:

"Oh! Look, Frank! A grave!"
By the side of the road, where the track from the top of the common crossed it at right angles and ran through a gate past the narrow wood, was a thin mound of turf, six feet by one,

with a moor-stone to the west, and on it someone had thrown a blackthorn spray and a handful of bluebells. Ashurst looked, and the poet in him moved. At crossroads—a suicide's grave! Poor mortals with their superstitions! (202)

This sighting sets going the story of Frank Ashurst, the mildly discontented, not quite middle-aged husband who "never looks for anything" but finds, in the course of the story, the memory of a lost passion. The frame story, about the day of the anniversary, is broken shortly by a core story, the "buried memory" that Ashurst recovers, and which arises after Ashurst, moved by the grave, has read a bit from "Murray's translation of the *Hippolytus*" and meditated on civilized man, the impossibility of eternal love, and the eternal glory of (Greek) art. The story of the memory—separated from the frame story by spaces and paragraph markings—is the story of a betrayal. Ashurst, before he was married, had stopped once on a journey at a country farm because of a lame football knee; had conquered the simple but passionate farm girl, Megan David, under an apple tree (attaining victory over a rival for her love); had promised to take her away with him; had left her, after some pangs of conscience, for Stella, the sophisticated but not quite so passionate, civilized, higher-class woman whom he eventually married. The exit from the memory, and from the inner story, finds him back at the crossroads, inquiring of the lame man about the mound. The man, a laborer he once knew on the farm (but who does not appear to recognize him), tells the story of a girl and of his discovery of her suicide by drowning. Ashurst, convinced that he has discovered the grave of Megan, walks off to meditate on the sad way in which his virtue has been rewarded, quotes to himself a few lines from a chorus in the *Hippolytus,* and returns to his wife, where he sees his sad plight in her painting.

The interest of this story in the context of *Civilization* is that it not only represents the roots of dissatisfaction in a narcissistic, "civilized" man in terms of a past, repressed memory, but shows his self-understanding, including his understanding of the memory, to involve a kind of misinterpretation, an erroneous reading of various texts in which he finds himself as a referent. This error is built into the structure of the plot in the two encounters with the grave, at the beginning and at the end: in the sighting of the grave and the hearing of its story. It is the connection of these two moments that constitutes the essential movement of the plot: Ashurst's recognition of his own story in the mark of the grave, his recognition of himself as a guilty being. This recognition is clearly characterized, however, not as true insight but as a form of narcissism: seeing himself in the grave is, for Ashurst, the inability to see others at all. The relation between Ashurst and the story of the lame man—who bears a specular relation to the earlier Ashurst whose story started with a lame football knee—thus represents something like the relation between ego and superego, a specular narcissism riddled by guilt and dissatisfaction.

It is on the figurative level that the ironization, or "analysis," of Ashurst's position is made possible for the reader: the pattern of loss and displacement represented by the relation between "Megan David" ("star of David" in Hebrew) [28] and "Stella" ("star" in Latin); between the apple blossoms of Megan's tree and the "apple-blossom coloring" of his wife's cheeks; between the "golden apples" for which Ashurst vainly longs and the "silver wedding-day" he must settle with. The loss and displacement of desire, linked to an impossible love of the past, a male rival, and a lost apple tree; the discovery through the encounter at a crossroads; and the literary allusions to *Hamlet* suggest that the root of Ashurst's guilt, the story he does *not* see, is one of a tabooed love and an incessant (fear of) castration. The story thus establishes a relation between a self-knowledge that takes the form of a repetition, a blindness, and a knowledge (that of psychoanalysis) which recuperates that repetition in the knowledge of another history.

These two forms of self-knowledge, that of civilized man and of psychoanalytic theory, come together in the reading of the *Hippolytus*, in the final lines that Ashurst quotes to himself:

"For mad is the heart of Love,
And gold the gleam of his wing;
And all to the spell thereof
Bend when he makes his spring.
All life that is wild and young
In mountain and wave and stream
All that of earth is sprung,
Or breathes in the red sunbeam;
Yea, and Mankind. O'er all a royal throne,
Cyprian, Cyprian, is thine alone!" (278)

For Ashurst, these lines show that "the Greek was right," that
love takes its sacrifices, that virtue cannot be rewarded in love—
a guilty as well as narcissistic thought in this case. But the lines,
for the psychoanalyst who knows his Greek plays, tell another
story: for they occur in the play just before the father, who has
exiled his son for a crime concerning the mother, confronts
him and watches him die. The lines, the psychoanalytic reader
knows, do not represent Ashurst's crime against Megan but an
older crime against himself: what Ashurst sees is the permanent loss in the object of love; what he doesn't see is the loss, or
castration, in himself. At the crossroads is not Megan but the
dead father, taking his revenge through the lame storyteller.

Before we too quickly take Ashurst's position and see the
story as an illustration of analytic theory, however, we might
take a closer look at the *Hippolytus*. This play has an added interest in this context because, in spite of its apparently Oedipal[29] configurations, it does not in fact replicate the plot of the
Oedipus Tyrranus but in many ways reverses it. The *Hippolytus*
tells the story of the punishment of Hippolytus by Aphrodite,
goddess of love, for his refusal to worship her as he does Artemis (goddess of the hunt). Aphrodite arranges, presumably,
the tragic events that lead to Hippolytus's death: his stepmother, Phaedra, who has fallen madly in love with him, reveals her love and is violently rejected; she hangs herself as a
consequence, leaving a note on her dead body which accuses
Hippolytus of the murder; the father Theseus, upon reading

the note, exiles Hippolytus, who is mangled by his own horses, and returns just in time for Theseus to learn of his error and watch his son die. Thus the plot presents, on one level, a negative reflection of *Oedipus:* rather than concerning the murder of a father by a son and his marriage to the mother, it concerns the son's rejection of the mother's love and a murder of the son by the father. But these reversals, more significantly, turn around a difference in the central structure of the plot—a plot which, in both plays, is focused on the process of discovery, of coming to know an event that has occurred in the past and off-stage; specifically, of producing a witness to a crime. The difference lies in the family: in *Oedipus* the murder victim, the dead around whose murder the discovery centers, is the father; in the *Hippolytus,* it is the mother. The interest of the *Hippolytus* in the context in which we find it is that it brings back, through the literary "illustration" of the central thesis of *Civilization,* the non-Oedipal mother. Or rather, the stepmother: when the mother returns in Freud's main theory, she returns somewhat changed—not as a true mother but as a stepmother, not as oceanic presence but as dead. It is through the figure of *this* mother—not nursing, but hanging—and the displacements she produces in the Oedipal triangle, that we may begin to understand the meaning of the mother's place in *Civilization.*

The lines that Ashurst quotes to himself seem to represent, we recall, a paradigmatically Oedipal configuration, the aggression between father and son over the mother. The play spends much time, indeed, on the specular, aggressive confrontation between Theseus and Hippolytus. This confrontation is characterized by a kind of identification and exchange of positions around the concept of "murderer," which begins when Hippolytus, accused of the murder of Phaedra by his father and banished as punishment, challenges him:

> By my faith, wert thou
> The son, and I the sire; and deemed I now
> In very truth thou hadst my wife assailed,
> I had not exiled thee, nor stood and railed,
> But lifted once mine arm, and struck thee dead![30]

Hippolytus's imaginary exchange of positions here with the father will become Theseus's tragic exchange of positions with his son when, at the son's death, the father identifies himself as the true murderer: "And my hand reeking from this thing!" (73). The principle of exchange which leads to this tragic death and self-recognition could be said to govern as well the relation between this tragic triangle and that of *Oedipus*, making of this particular action of the *Hippolytus* the second story already implied in the other play.

The tragic exchange of positions between Theseus and Hippolytus depends, however, on a larger irony which Theseus's self-recognition as "murderer" doesn't fully grasp. This comes out in Artemis's revelation of the true story behind Phaedra's murderer:

> And then Phaedra, panic-eyed
> Wrote a false writ, and slew thy son, and died . . .
> Thy fault, O king, its ignorance sunders wide
> From very wickedness; and she who died
> By death the more disarmed thee, making dumb
> The voice of question. (68) [31]

The truth of Artemis's story is not only that it isn't Hippolytus who murdered Phaedra, nor simply that Phaedra murdered herself, but that Phaedra, in committing suicide and leaving a "false writ," in effect "slew" Hippolytus. The father's act of aggression has been the tool of the mother's. This is emphasized moreover by the implication that in killing Hippolytus Phaedra also "disarmed" Theseus: the phallic confrontation between father and son has been merely the result of a previous castration of the father by the mother. The tables are turned on the Oedipal configuration: the aggressive revenge of the father on the son for the mother is in fact determined by the revenge of the mother. The "pre-Oedipal" mother functions neither as an object of desire, nor as oceanic presence, but as an aggressive effect.

This position of the mother, and her aggressive "act," are not comparable to either of the male positions. For any "real" action she may have taken is only against herself, in her suicide, and this takes place off-stage (indeed like the murder of Laius). The way in which Phaedra is present to the two men is, rather, as a dead body and a text, an inscribed tablet attached to a corpse. The confrontation of the two men—neither of whom, incidentally, meet Phaedra face to face in the play—will be produced by the encounter with this corpse and this writing. The interpretation of this double "evidence" will entirely determine the positions of the two men in relation to each other. The effect of the mother will be the consequence of a reading.

In the first fatal confrontation of Theseus and his son, their positions are formulated in terms of their understanding of the cause of the mother's death. Against the father's accusation, Hippolytus argues that he has not killed her, that he has never touched her, indeed that women (as a whole) are essentially nonexistent for him. The mother, Hippolytus claims, was never even present for him in the first place. The relation between father and son around the dead mother thus resembles, as we recall, the two supplementary stories of *Civilization*, that is, the two different father-son relations.[32] In the one case, the father was never really there, and the self-division within the son was thus a matter of mere figuration; in the other case, the father was murdered, and the self-division was a reference to this event. In the *Hippolytus*, these two positions are reiterated around the body of the dead mother, but with a difference: the dead mother is not just dead but a text; she is not just a body but also an inscribed tablet. If the difference between the two stories in *Civilization* depends on the interpretation of death, this difference is seen to rely, in the *Hippolytus*, on the interpretation, also, of an inscription. The mother's function is to add to the sign of death, to the corpse (a sign read as a mere figure by Hippolytus, read referentially by Theseus), something else to be read, a piece of writing.

It is the effect of this difference that will bring the positions of the two men into a kind of exchange which underlies but also undoes the tragic exchange, the tragic irony of their specular reversals. This maternal effect is felt, first of all, in the form the father-son confrontation takes at its central moment, as they argue about the accusation that Theseus bases on the mother's tablet. Theseus and Hippolytus confront each other here, not over the truth or falsehood of the accusation, but rather over the authority of the body/text as a witness. The question concerns the figure of the speaking subject which gives voice to the accusation. It is a question of the authority of this text as a subject, a witness, expressed in a highly legal language. The climax comes after Theseus has argued that the tablet bears witness against Hippolytus, whose own oaths have no power against it:

Hippolytus
Ye stones, will ye not speak? Ye castle walls!
Bear witness if I be so vile, so false!

Theseus
Aye, fly to voiceless witnesses! Yet here
A dumb deed speaks against thee, and speaks clear! (56)

Hippolytus's apostrophe to the walls suggests indirectly that Theseus's use of the body and the tablet as witness is nothing more than an apostrophe to an inanimate object: it is an arbitrary act of figuration which is as authoritative as an apostrophe to a wall. The mother, that is, has authority only as an arbitrary act of figuration entirely independent of any empirical reference. Theseus's reply insists, figuratively, that the witnessing is based in a real deed, referred to by the tablet and body. The authority of the witness is constituted by the referential function of body and text, in the function of her death as a reference to the act that murdered her. Theseus argues for the mother's death not as the impossibility of truth, but as truth's very voice.

The language in which Theseus insists on the referential authority of the mother, moreover, does not eliminate figure, but involves a curious elision and refiguration of the mother which brings it in close relation to the odd figurations of the primal father. In Theseus's antithesis, one would expect "voice-less witnesses" (ἀφώνος μάρτυρας) to be opposed directly to "the mother's voice," speaking figuratively through her body and text. But the witness Theseus produces is instead a "dumb deed" (ἔργον οὐλεγον). This focuses the antithesis, oddly, on "voiceless" and "dumb": if the walls cannot bear witness because they are voiceless, the deed, implicitly, can bear witness because it is "dumb." It is in this *speaking dumbness* that the mother appears. For the deed speaks, in Theseus's language, through the elision of the mother and the deed's assumption of her attributes; the life of the *deed* is the form of the dead mother. The mother thus bears witness as the personification of the very deed by which she is eliminated. This metaleptic position is precisely that of the dead father in the primal father story. The authority of the voice comes from the act which speaks, which speaks through the figure of the death it is conjectured to have produced.

Theseus thus distinguishes himself from Hippolytus through the referential authority of the figure of the dead mother, a difference he emphasizes by responding to the poetic apostrophe of his son with a more strictly legal language. But in an earlier passage, when he is alone with the corpse, Theseus himself will use precisely the apostrophe he here rejects. In the earlier passage, however, the emphasis is not on the connection of the act with the murderer, but on the connection of the tablet with the body:

> **Theseus**
> Ha, what is this that hangs from her dear hand?
> A tablet! It would make me understand
> Some dying wish, some charge about her bed
> and children. 'Twas the last prayer, ere her head
> Was bowed forever. [Taking the tablet]
> Fear not, my lost bride,
> No woman born shall lie at Theseus' side,
> Nor rule in Theseus' house!
> A seal! Ah, see
> How her gold signet here looks up at me,

> Trustfully. Let me tear this thread away,
> And read what tale the tablet seeks to say. (45)

The connection Theseus will make between the accusation, the words of the tablet, and the subject "Phaedra" begins here, as the link between the dead hand (in the first line) and the speaking tablet (in the last). This link is made possible, first of all, by the figure (Theseus's apostrophe) that turns the actual link between body and tablet into the relation between *Phaedra* and her *message*. It is the apostrophe which opens the space of the voice. Yet we notice that it is not exactly Phaedra's voice, at the end, which speaks, but rather that of the tablet. And not the tablet as the *words* of the tablet, which have not yet been read, but of the tablet *itself*, as the potential for the meaning within it. The apostrophe, in a sense, falls between the dead body and the words of the tablet; it falls upon the link between them, the gold band or more accurately the nonverbal inscription upon it.[33] What Theseus "reads" is nothing other than this bare link, this articulating mark, which has no meaning in itself yet irresistibly demands to be read as the intentional relation between a subject and a meaning, between Phaedra and the reference of her words. The gold band is not unlike the articulating marks of any language (as syntax, grammar, punctuation) which makes possible meaning (as intention) and yet cannot be said, for sure, to be itself intended as meaningful.

The apostrophe that decides in favor of this latter intention is not a "mere" figure, however, because it is not imposed upon an absence but called for, commanded as it were, by a mark. The reading is imposed by the question of the mark, the question mark raised by the inscription: is this a text, or just a mark? Or: can this be read as a sign? The apostrophe is thus neither completely arbitrary (as figure), nor entirely determined (as reference), but the figure by which the very distinction between the two, as a distinction dependent upon the "sign," is made possible in the first place. The "law" of this figure, the imperative it speaks, is precisely the double impossibility and necessity of deciding on the significatory status of the articulating mark, the marks upon which language depends (but which are not thereby dependable signs), on deciding whether the mark means at all. It is this uncertainty which is presented in the play by the fact that there is neither *just* a text nor *just* a body, but both a text and a body.[34]

Theseus and Hippolytus face each other around this double fact as the distinction and immediate confusion of two positions—the mother already dead, the mother being killed—in the slippage between mark and sign. This slippage is represented, moreover, through the transformation of the figure of gold: if the gold signet links Phaedra and text as a mere mark, neither presence nor absence but inscription, it is rather the gold apples of the Hesperides which will appear in the play's central chorus ("the apple tree, the singing and the gold") as a figure of loss, the lost object of love, the ever-receding referent which is always necessarily a figure. The golden band is lost, or rather found, in the lost love of the ancient garden. This would suggest, moreover, that the plot of the play itself repeats this slippage: that the death of Phaedra is not so much an event that *succeeds* and results from her love of and rejection by Hippolytus, but that the love story is in a sense invented in order to account for the death, or rather for the corpse and text it discovers at its center—that the plot allegorizes the error of the apostrophic reading. One might say, in addition, that, as it is translated by Murray, the story of Phaedra's (off-stage) hanging stages Theseus's own first question upon discovery of the tablet, "What is this that *hangs* from her dear hand?"[35]

The representation of this error by the plot would be suggested, moreover, by the fact that, regardless of what we may want to say about Phaedra's love, it is not so much the love but the anger, the wrath of the goddess of love which sets the action of the play in motion. And this wrath is the response to the attempt by Hippolytus to worship only one goddess, the goddess of the hunt, represented with Aphrodite on the stage as a statue (Eros and Thanatos?): Hippolytus, in choosing to worship, to apostrophize only one goddess, to maintain only one position in his relation to the statue, ends up being entirely determined by the position he has excluded. But the "allegory" of this confusion of father and son which makes the plot of the play is itself not to be considered, merely as a figure, as a figure "only" of a reading. For it is from this other place, the place of the voice he refuses to read, that the name of his *true* mother is spoken; it is Aphrodite who reminds us, at the opening, that the mother of Hippolytus is not the one who kills herself off-stage but the "Amazon" who never comes on stage at all.[36]

The psychoanalytic reader of "The Apple Tree" finds himself in a similar position.[37] For the power of this analytic reading depends, as does Ashurst's, on the reading of a mark as a sign, by assigning a meaning to the grave. This is in fact, as we recall, not first of all a grave at a crossroads, but a "mound," "by the side of the road": a mark that indeed demands to be read, though it is of uncertain meaning in itself. It is the reading of this mark which, while permitting the remembering of the past, forgets the material breaks that always put into question the meaningfulness of the significant links between frame story and inner story (marked by a space and a number); and this forgetting, necessary for the *reader*, is also, for him, the discovery of golden apples, the reading of the gold as the loss which is the meaning of the story, the meaningful connection of the text *beside* the main text, the epigraph which precedes the story:

> "The apple-tree, the singing and the gold."
> Murray's "Hippolytus of Euripides"[38]

The analytic reader's position, against Ashurst's narcissistic interpretation of the play, depends first of all upon the reader's reading of the link between epigraph and text—the reading of the word *gold*, which is like Theseus's apostrophe of the gold band. This is also, we are reminded here, akin to the movement by which "the Greek" is translated into modern times, an eternal truth, by "Murray."[39] Greek and English, past and nostalgic present are represented again as a textual relation, a juxtaposition of texts not entirely free yet never determinately related to one another—a relation that is rediscovered, as we find, in the significant connection of the ancient Hebrew, "Megan David" (star of David) and the more recent Latin, "Stella" (star). Who can say where the subject, the woman, the ancient mother resides in this translation? Her voice would seem to arise precisely in her lack of place, in the opening up of the possibility of the place of meaning. For if the grave is given a meaning by the lame man, whose story captures the conscience of Frank, it is not the lame man but the wife, not the specular double but the voice *beside* Frank that first opens up the space of reference, that sees the meaning of the mound, or more accurately, that *commands* Frank *to look:* "Oh! Look, Frank! A grave!"

The mother cannot be said to have a *place* in the Galsworthy story, then, but a voice that speaks in the imperative to read the relation, the articulation of the epigraph and the text beneath it. Similarly, the Galsworthy citation in Freud's footnote reintroduces the "mother" into the theoretical text of *Civilization* not only *within* the story, but in the necessity of finding a relation between the footnote and the text above it. The meaning of the mother, insofar as she enters the theory, resides in the meaningfulness of this articulation, which is also the relation between theory and literature, *Historie* and *Roman*.

This relation can first be read in terms of an exchange of history and story, or of the "literal" meaning of the theory and its "figuration" in narrative. For the story, which figuratively illustrates the theory, suddenly reappears in the middle of the theory itself. Or rather, it reappears in the story *of* the theory, the history of the drive theory provided in chapter 6 of *Civilization*.[40] Here Freud tells us how the death drive was first conceptualized in psychoanalytic theory. The first steps toward the concept, he says, were hypothetical:

> The phenomena of life could be explained from the concurrent or mutually opposing action of [Eros and Thanatos]. It was not easy, however, to demonstrate the activities of this supposed

> death instinct. The manifestations of Eros were conspicuous
> and noisy enough. It might be assumed that the death instinct
> operated dumbly [*stumm*] within the organism towards its dis-
> solution, but that, of course, was no proof. A more fruitful idea
> was that a portion of the instinct is diverted towards the exter-
> nal world and comes to light as an instinct of aggressiveness and
> destructiveness. (119, translation modified)

Freud remembers that, in theory, the death drive was always
dumb. This memory refers us to a moment in an earlier text,
The Ego and the Id, where the insight into the death drive was
formulated as follows: "We are driven to conclude that the
death instincts are by their nature dumb [*stumm*] and that the
clamour of life proceeds for the most part from Eros."[41] "A
dumb deed speaks against thee," Freud says to the guilty psyche. The formulation of the *theoretical* concept is made in a
kind of confrontation with the psyche, an accusation by theory
of the self that recalls Theseus's accusation of his son. But there
is also a footnote to Freud's line, in which we read:

> In fact, on our view it is through the agency of Eros that the
> destructive instincts that are directed towards the external
> world have been diverted from the self.[42]
>
> (*Nach unserer Auffassung sind ja die nach aussen gerichteten
> Destruktionstriegbe durch Vermittlung des Eros vom eigenen Selbst
> abgelenkt werden.*)

The deed of aggression toward others is revealed to be the
effect of aggression toward the self, an act which is never seen
or known as such, except insofar as it fails, that is, insofar as it
is turned toward others through the intervention of Eros.[43]
The act takes place off-stage, as it were, and appears only in its
effects on others, an appearance resulting from the work of
"love." Can we not recognize in this story the drama of the
mother's suicide, causing the tragedy of aggression between father and son? The "turning outward" of the mother's aggression would thus describe the error by which the text and body

of the mother are read as the sign of a murder, the apostrophe of the mark as a sign of meaning. The theory and the story are indistinguishable.[44]

And yet, Freud's story of the "truth" of the off-stage scene (like Artemis's intervention in the play), his knowledge of the dumb act of suicidal aggression, occurs *not* in the main text, *in* the theory, but in a footnote. The "literary" element of the footnote cannot be located *in* the theory without already reading the relation, again, between the main text and a note beneath it. In introducing the footnote here Freud reintroduces the problem of articulation which the theory is supposed to *know* as Eros and Thanatos. In order to *understand* the relation between Eros and Thanatos, we have to read the break between text and note, to assign a meaning to the number that marks the spot, the point at which the two texts are joined. If the death drive is "directed" (*gerichtet*) outward by Eros, the concept of "Eros" in *Civilization* is established (*aufgerichtet*) through reference to the note; if the death drive here is "diverted" (*abgelenkt*) through Eros, could we not say that the full concept of "Eros" hangs (*ist aufgehenkt*), as it were, upon the mark of the "note"? The "mother" speaks here, as a necessary error of theory, not in the *impossibility* of its literal meaning—in its figurative dimension—but in the very *necessity* of its meaning in the first place, in the failure of its articulations *not to mean*. The theory of aggression as the failure of suicide, as the error in which the self acquires meaning, is itself subject to the error by which the articulating mark is read as a sign of meaning. Psychoanalysis witnesses the truth of the self only insofar as it repeats the error it uncovers.

It is as witness to this action, then, that the mother also enters chapter 7, as the link between the two stories—the story of the origins of the superego, in the individual and in the race. The insistence on both stories, as we recall, was a kind of critical self-awareness of theory, the movement between a theory of the psyche as autonomous figuration and a critique of that theory as a kind of literalization. The murder of the primal father was a form of reflection of the theory on itself. But the appearance of the mother as the link between the two stories, between the theory of the psyche and the theory of theory, tells another story, a kind of forgetting that necessarily takes place in this theoretical self-reflection. The appearance of the mother by the side of the father tells us that the impossible imperative to choose between the two stories—the critical tension of the theory—itself stands under another imperative, the imperative of meaning. The movement to the third story (which is a kind of third party, a neighbor of sorts) is the return of reference which is grounded neither in the perceived world, nor in mere figuration, but in the figuring of the mark as a sign—the sign of "love."[45] Thus if the theory of the father remembers the origin of the psyche, the mother is the sign of what it must necessarily forget. What chapter 7 ultimately tells us is the impossibility of remembering the origin without repeating its forgetting.

In the eventful forgetting of *Civilization*, a witness speaks. Its truth, however, is not in what it remembers but in how its forgetting gives voice to a memory.

> **Theseus**
> Doth not the tablet cry aloud, yea, shriek,
> Things not to be forgotten?
> > (Murray's "Hippolytus of Euripides," trans. of line 876)
>
> βοαῖ βοαῖ δέλτος ἄλαστα
> (Woe, woe, tablet not to be forgotten)
> > (Euripides, Hippolytus, line 876)

CONCLUSION

Mourning Experience

 How covetous the Mind is to be furnished with all such *Ideas* . . . may be a little guess'd, by what is observable in Children new-born, who always turn their eyes to that part, from whence the Light comes, lay them how you please.

Locke, *An Essay Concerning Human Understanding* (II.9.7)

Thus the *Ideas*, as well as Children, of our Youth, often die before us: And our Minds represent to us those Tombs, to which we are approaching; where though the Brass and Marble remain, yet the Inscriptions are effaced by time, and the Imagery moulders away.

Locke, *Essay* (II.10.5)

Surely one has no choice but to be an empiricist so far as one's theory of linguistic meaning is concerned.

W. V. O. Quine, "Epistemology Naturalized"[1]

The latent project of the present volume has been to open up the possibility of a rethinking of empiricism in order to attempt to understand anew the critical traditions that are defined in terms of it. In the prevailing understanding of these traditions, which is based on the explicit claims of the texts that constitute their corpus, English empiricism (of which Locke is one of the main writers) is often represented as the less sophisticated origin of self-reflection, which Romantic poetry, on the one hand, and critical philosophy, on the other, reject or overcome. What both of the later traditions respond to, in this view, is a particular notion of origin which determines the Lockean—or the classical empiricist—understanding of understanding: the idea that we can know our knowledge by tracing it to its origins in the sensory world. This notion of self-understanding not only seems to derive thought from the empirical world but makes self-understanding a matter of mere observation, like the chronicling of a natural phenomenon, bound entirely to the laws of physical perception. For later writers such as Kant and Wordsworth, this apparently simple notion of empirical origin will not account adequately for the power of thought to turn upon itself, to detach itself from the laws of the empirical world. English Romantic poetry and German critical philosophy claim, in different ways, to overcome empirical shortcomings by replacing the observed empirical origin with a kind of lack or absence, a fundamental break with, or detachment from, sensory reality, which is what makes possible the turn of the mind upon itself.

Following the individual forms of this claim to transcend empiricism, the present book has first shown how they all involve, explicitly or implicitly, a certain theory of language. Wordsworth can, in this perspective, be viewed as replacing a literalized language of empiricism, in particular the vocabulary of sensation, with a figurative language of "imagination," substituting a "Romantic," figurative narrative for the literal empiricist's tracing of origins. The power of imaginative self-consciousness which springs from a lack rests precisely on the power of figurative language to free itself from the constraints of literal, referential meaning, or a meaning grounded in a direct, perceivable link between language and the empirical world.

In Kant, the philosophical critique of empiricism also, ultimately, rests on the implicit recognition that empirical reference cannot be the basis of conceptual self-understanding. The replacement of a philosophy aimed at knowing—by referring directly to—things in the world, with a philosophy aimed at knowing the limits of knowledge, is made possible by the self-reflecting capacity of "symbolic" language. In this case, reference to the world is subordinated to a kind of self-reference, and the power of thought to turn upon itself is grounded in the self-representing power of the symbol. The symbol becomes the basis of Kant's entire philosophical system, an elaborate, self-reflecting structure called the "architectonic." In this view of the relation between Locke and the later authors, then, Wordsworth's narrative and Kant's system are indeed linked in the common priority they attribute to self-reference, or to figure over reference. Read in this context, the scene of mourning, the facing of the dead parent or child at the very origin, could point to a possible dramatization of a referential absence which grounds meaning, something like a nothingness speaking at the heart of language.

The process of interpretation opened up by these texts does not end, however, with the texts' conceptual or thematic wish to move beyond empiricism. A closer reading of their formal textual structures has lead the present work to reevaluate the very claim to transcend empiricism as itself not merely a conceptual design but a rhetorical and narrative gesture which, as such, can be interpreted—and questioned—in its own right. The argument I here advance is that such questioning, precisely, is already present at the very locus of empiricism, and that it addresses us rhetorically and narratively, from within Locke's *Essay,* through the appearance of the absent child. In the attempt to define empirical sanity against its mad other— the madman who forgets his empirical origins—Locke's text comes up against the hallucination of remembering—the madness of the mother endlessly mourning her dead child. Inhabiting empiricism, the face of this dead child signifies a lack at the heart of empirical reality, but a lack that can by no means be equated with a simple loss of empirical or referential truth. Rather than a figuration free from reference, the child embodies a reminder of, precisely, something that must be forgotten at the heart of reference, a figure equally unsubsumable by either empirical or by critical thinking. To read Locke's child is thus to reread (to rethink) the language of empiricism, and hence to reread (to rethink) the languages of Romanticism and of critical philosophy insofar as they are both defined through their opposition to the language of empiricism. I have argued, in this sense, that the texts here studied do not represent a simple "overcoming" of empiricism—as the simple remembering of a past error—but that their textuality rather enacts both their memory and their transcendence of empiricism as the repetition of a forgetting. It is as though the texts themselves embodied something like a "mad" remembering which is neither fully knowledge nor fully its lack.

What in my view is so compelling in these authors is that they refuse to leave us with the reassuring negativity of loss; they show us, rather, how, on the one hand, the locating of this loss is the very aim of thought and the very origin of its power, and how not-knowing, on the other hand, is both constitutive of negative thinking and also, fundamentally, disruptive of it.

Freud's text, at this point, marks the moment in which the narrative effects of this conceptual movement form the modern understanding of the self. For the concept of conflicted, or partially unconscious, sexuality will now represent the tension between the predictability of the structure of psychical figures (Oedipal love and Oedipal rivalry)—the possibility of a universal theory of psychoanalytic figures unconstrained by the immediacy of present referents—and a fundamental resistance of particular stories to theoretical abstraction, the impossibility of separating any individual life from the particularity of its past. Freud's odd "empiricism"—the location of actual events (the murder of the primal father) in a literal "pre-history" of humanity—can be rethought through the renewed understanding I have proposed here of empiricism, as an insistence of reference that is not, however, simply grounded in, and subsumed by, the empirical world. Civilized sexuality, as the conflicted or guilty confrontation of the individual and the superego, is the new "experience" of this double bind, an experience that no longer coincides with the notion of experience which, reading Locke traditionally, we thought we knew. The power of Freud's text is, precisely, that we cannot read the death(s) of the parent(s) represented in it as mere fantasmatic figures, that we cannot simply understand our "lives," as they are referred to in Freud's text, in terms of a universal structure free of referential constraints: in Freud, our lives return, indeed, with an "experiential" force far greater than would be permitted by any conventional empiricism. This return occurs as the unconsciousness both of the "experience" and of the psychoanalytic argument. The return of "empiricism" occurs, in other words, as what the text, precisely, cannot fully know, but what it represents, in the encounter of parent and child, as its very origin.

It is significant, then, that the pattern which emerges over the four chapters at the same time marks the recurrence of a narrative of radical loss and the continual displacement of the object or the agent of the loss: in Locke, it is the mother who mourns her dead child, while in Wordsworth it is the child who mourns the dead mother; in Kant it is the father who murders the son, while in Freud it is the sons who murder the father. It would be tempting to try to understand these apparent symmetries—within a tradition in which authors both reflect upon and respond to one another—as the inevitable movements of a dialectical process, and as the continual reversal of the grounds of knowledge in the subject and in the object. Each text does indeed contain, as I have shown, in the very movement of its argument, a dialectical dimension that permits it to be read, precisely, over and against itself. To this extent, the resemblances and the reversals in these now familiar scenes do reveal a universal possibility, and a logic of a possible conceptual freedom from experience.

Yet the points of exchange of the positions of the mourning scene in Wordsworth and in Locke, and of the scene of murder in Kant and in Freud, while apparently transparent to interpretation, nevertheless remain opaque to understanding. It has also been the burden of my argument to mark the ways in which the singular power of each text exceeds the symmetries that can be drawn between them, and leaves a referential residue which cannot simply be reclaimed by either a conceptual or a figurative logic.

It is this return of reference which the preceding chapters try to trace in the return of the narrative of death through the diversity of the attempts to move beyond the doctrine of empiricism. In the scenes of mourning and of murder, the referential moment reappears, precisely, in opposition to the thematic or doctrinal aspects of the texts, as a resistance to the very effort of empirical conceptualization and as a disruption of the very effort at *understanding loss*.

The thrust of the present study has thus been to try to *think together* both the concept of experience and the critique of the concept of experience, both empiricism and the claim—or the design—to transcend empiricism. The claims of empiricism— of experience as it might be bound together with knowledge and language in philosophy, literature, or psychoanalytic inquiry—have been shown to point back to that recurring moment in the text in which understanding—in itself uncannily embodied in the figure of the death of a child or of a parent— tries to trace and know its origins, but instead repeatedly reoriginates in a referential movement of forgetting.

But the way in which experience leaves something *unclaimed, either* by empiricism *or* by its critique, is perhaps what most profoundly defines both the persistence of empiricism and the claims to its transcendence, both the singular survival of experience and the ineluctability of its endless mourning.

NOTES

1 The Face of Experience

1. There is very little work that pays close attention to Locke's concept of association. This is evident from a brief glance at Roland Hall and Roger Woolhouse's *Eighty Years of Locke Scholarship: A Bibliographical Guide* (Edinburgh: Edinburgh University Press, 1983). This work lists only twenty works in the last eighty years which involve extended discussions of the chapter on association. Of these, seven are general histories of psychology, concerned primarily with the empirical tradition as the basis of modern empirical techniques, and three are on *Tristram Shandy*. Several works do prove exceptions to the general rule; of particular note is Ernest Lee Tuveson, "The New Epistemology," in his *The Imagination as a Means of Grace: Locke and the Aesthetics of Romanticism* (Berkeley: University of California Press, 1960). Other helpful discussions are to be found in David Rapaport, "Locke: The Borderland of Sensualism and Empiricism," in his *The History of the Concept of Association of Ideas* (New York: International Universities Press, 1974), and G. S. Brett, "British Psychologists," in his *A History of Psychology*, vol. 2 (London: George Allen & Unwin, 1921).

2. Contemporary philosophers have recognized the many problems surrounding the naming and classifying of philosophical groups, and some of them have put into question the simple identification of Locke as the "father" or founder of empiricism, often preferring to allocate that role to Hobbes and to link Locke more closely with Descartes and Malebranche. (The question of associationism in particular, as I have suggested, has received less attention.) The work of Michael Ayers and Daniel Garber has been particularly helpful in expanding our perspectives on Locke. Nonetheless, the idea of Locke as the founder and main representative of empiricism has had an influ-

ence in the history of thought which is interesting in its own right, and has by no means been entirely eradicated from contemporary thinking. On the illusions of traditional histories of philosophy, and the problems of identifying groups such as the empiricists, see Jonathan Ree, Michael Ayers, and Adam Westoby, *Philosophy and Its Past* (Sussex, England: Harvester Press, 1978), and R. S. Woolhouse, "Introduction" to *The Empiricists* (New York: Oxford University Press, 1988).

3. Some of the strongest representations of this position can be found in Walter Jackson Bate, *From Classic to Romantic: Premises of Taste in Eighteenth-Century England* (New York: Harper & Row, 1946); Basil Willey, "On Wordsworth and the Locke Tradition," in *The Seventeenth Century Background* (London: Chatto & Windus, 1950); and M. H. Abrams, *The Mirror and the Lamp: Romantic Theory and the Critical Tradition* (Oxford: Oxford University Press, 1953). For versions of the "negative" relation see A. C. Bradley, *English Poetry and German Philosophy in the Age of Wordsworth*, The Adamson Lecture, 1909 (Manchester: Manchester University Press, 1909); Earl R. Wasserman, "The English Romantics: The Grounds of Knowledge," in *Studies in Romanticism* vol. 4 (1964); Alfred Cobban, *Edmund Burke and the Revolt against the Eighteenth Century*, 2d ed. (London: George Allen & Unwin, 1960). On the "positive" relation see Warren Beatty, *William Wordsworth: His Doctrine and Art in Their Historical Relations* (Madison: University of Wisconsin Press, 1922)—this focuses primarily on Wordsworth's relation to Hartley; for the "transcendence" version see John A. Hodgson, *Wordsworth's Philosophical Poetry, 1797–1814* (Lincoln: University of Nebraska Press, 1980), and Alan Grob, *The Philosophic Mind: A Study of Wordsworth's Poetry and Thought, 1797–1805* (Columbia: Ohio State University Press, 1973). Two works that attempt to reposition Locke in the tradition are Paul de Man, "The Epistemology of Metaphor," in Sheldon Sacks, ed., *On Metaphor* (Chicago: University of Chicago Press, 1978), and Hans Aarsleff, *From Locke to Saussure: Essays on the Study of Language and Intellectual History* (Minneapolis: University of Minnesota Press, 1982). An interesting rereading of Hartley, which takes into account the "literary" features of his *Observations on Man,* is offered by Jerome Christensen in *Coleridge's Blessed Machine of Language* (Ithaca: Cornell University Press, 1981).

4. This may occur in studies concerned with the "philosophy" of a poet in context, in which case there is a fairly explicit interpretation of empiricism at work; but numerous other studies, most frequently on Coleridge and Wordsworth, rely on an implicit understanding of am experiential vocabulary, particularly when reading passages that

seem to thematize experiential immediacy. See for example Melvin Rader, *Wordsworth: A Philosophical Approach* (Oxford: Clarendon Press, 1967), and K. M. Wheeler, *The Creative Mind in Coleridge's Poetry* (London: Heinemann, 1981).

5. See for example the discussion of the "Blessed Babe" passage in Frances Ferguson, *Wordsworth: Language as Counter-Spirit* (New Haven: Yale University Press, 1977), and Richard J. Onorato, *The Character of the Poet: Wordsworth in the Prelude* (Princeton: Princeton University Press, 1971).

6. From "On the Principles of Genial Criticism," in *Biographia Literaria* (Book Two). Coleridge had a good deal to do with the myth of a "reductive" empiricism which he and Wordsworth left behind. An extended polemic against Locke is contained in letters 381–84 of the *Collected Letters of Samuel Taylor Coleridge*, ed. Earl Leslie Griggs (Oxford: Clarendon Press, 1956–71).

7. Quotations of Locke are from John Locke, *An Essay Concerning Human Understanding*, ed. Peter H. Nidditch (Oxford: Clarendon Press, 1975), based on the 1700 edition. Book, chapter, and paragraph numbers are indicated in parentheses in the text.

8. The claims to self-limitation are, for example, similar in some respects to Kant's assertions in the preface to the second edition of the *Critique of Pure Reason*. An interesting study would examine the differences between the use of "limit" in each. On the notion of the limit in Locke see François Duchesneau, *L'empirisme de Locke* (The Hague: Martinus Nijhoff, 1973), pp. 253–45, and Nicholas Jolley, *Leibniz and Locke: A Study of the New Essays on Human Understanding* (New York: Oxford University Press, 1984), p. 3.

9. The complexity of this classification has been noted in footnote 2, above. Those interested in exploring the many "non-empiricist" philosophical strands in Locke can consult Reinhard Brandt, ed., *John Locke: Symposium Wolfenbüttel 1979* (New York: Walter de Gruyter, 1981); J. L. Mackie, *Problems from Locke* (New York: Oxford University Press, 1976); and I. D. Tipton, ed., *Locke on Human Understanding: Selected Essays* (New York: Oxford University Press, 1977). The relation between Locke and philosophers who are not considered to be part of the empirical tradition does not eliminate the significance of Locke's emphasis on "experience" as a fundamental characteristic of his philosophical doctrine and of the form his arguments take.

10. H. E. Matthews notes that both Locke and Malebranche include under the heading of "perception" both "intellectual insight" as well as "sense-perception." See "Locke, Malebranche, and the Representative Theory," in Tipton, *Locke on Human Understanding*.

11. This is the subject of Book One of the *Essay,* which refers in part to the so-called "Cambridge Platonists." On Locke's arguments concerning innate ideas, and the views he was contesting, see Mackie, *Problems from Locke,* pp. 206–7, and J. W. Yolton, *John Locke and the Way of Ideas* (New York: Oxford University Press, 1956), chap. 2.

12. These are the terms Locke assigns the two sources of ideas in chapter 1.

13. This viewpoint has of course been held by others apart from literary critics; I am particularly interested, however, in how this view has affected the interpretation of Romantic literature.

14. Abrams, *The Mirror and the Lamp,* p. 57.

15. It is interesting that the sensationist interpretation is sometimes connected with a view of Locke as *un*knowledgeable in matters of physics. Locke's physical model for thought is said to derive from Boyle and from Locke's experience as a physician, rather than from an understanding of Newton. See for example David Givner, "Scientific Preconceptions in Locke's Philosophy of Language" in *Journal of the History of Ideas* 23 (1962). That Locke not only read Newton carefully but was instrumental in establishing the reputation of the *Principia* is argued by James L. Axtell in "Locke, Newton, and the Two Cultures," in John W. Yolton, ed., *John Locke: Problems and Perspectives: A Collection of New Essays* (Cambridge: Cambridge University Press, 1969). Locke's refusal to introduce a more mathematical or technical physical vocabulary into his *Essay* suggests an awareness of the distinction between his discursive, philosophical work and "natural philosophy," a distinction that a sensationalist interpretation tends to miss. Of particular significance in this context is what Locke has to say about the nondefinable names of "simple ideas" such as "motion" and "light"; here the problem of using discursive systems to understand the empirical world is a central problem. In the summary Locke wrote for a student of Newtonian physics, *Elements of Natural Philosophy,* the opening definition of motion immediately raises the same problem: "Motion is so well known by the sight and touch, that to use words to give a clearer idea of it, would be in vain." The difficulties raised by the introduction of the word *force,* which were so important to Kant's critical philosophy, are also implicitly acknowledged by the nondefinition Locke offers of this word: "It appears, as far as human observation reaches, to be a settled law of nature, that 'all bodies have a tendency, attraction, or gravitation towards one another.'" See *The Elements of Natural Philosophy, to which is added Some Thoughts Concerning Reading and Study for a Gentleman* (Whitehaven: W. Sheperd, 1714). Locke's sensitivity to the problems of a scientific vocabulary in-

dicates that his own vocabulary of sensation should not be reduced too quickly.

16. The attempt to distinguish Locke from simple sensationism and even to question his status as an empiricist has also been a project of some recent philosophers, as I noted above (footnote 2).

17. Rapaport, *The History of the Concept of Association of Ideas*, p. 71.

18. Tuveson, *The Imagination as a Means of Grace*, p. 20.

19. On Hobbes's concept of motion see Thomas A. Spragens, Jr., *The Politics of Motion: The World of Thomas Hobbes* (Lexington: University Press of Kentucky, 1973); Adrienne Donald has suggested a phantasmatic aspect to Hobbes's concept of motion in *Wordsworth and the Relation of Philosophy and Poetry in Britain* (unpublished manuscript). On Hartley see Christensen, *Coleridge's Blessed Machine of Language*.

20. The failed attempt to establish a confluence of "literal" meaning with a reference to a physical world may be considered one of the identifying characteristics of empirical texts.

21. These principles emerge more clearly in a passage in which Locke comments on his own terminology of conveyance:

> First, *Our Senses*, conversant about particular sensible Objects, do *convey into the Mind*, several distinct *Perceptions* of things, according to those various ways, wherein those Objects do affect them: And thus we come by those *Ideas*, we have of *Yellow*, *White*, *Heat*, *Cold*, *Soft*, *Hard*, *Bitter*, *Sweet*, and all those which we call sensible qualities, which when I say the senses convey into the mind, I mean, they from external Objects convey into the mind what produces there those *Perceptions*. (II.1.3)

The addition of the phrase "what produces" in order to explain the concept of conveyance specifies the conveying as physical, but only by shifting the burden of passage from body to mind onto the word *produces*. In the chapter on cause and effect, this word is used to define causation: "That which produces any simple or complex *Idea*, we denote by the general Name *Cause*; and that which is produced, *Effect*" (II.26.1). The specification of conveying as carrying "what produces" mental perceptions thus indicates that what is hidden in the use of *convey* is a barely articulated causal principle, which, crossing the barrier between body and mind, is as enigmatic as the motion of conveyance. The causal account of sensation ultimately leaves aside its empirical basis and returns to the analogy between eye and understanding.

22. This is in the third book, "Of Words."

23. It could be argued that the confusion of causal and descriptive narratives is one of the problems Kant attempts to avoid in his critical conception of causality.

24. This kind of argument thus differs from an analysis such as, for example, Hegel's analysis of "Sense-Certainty" in *The Phenomenology of Spirit*.

25. This is not to say that perception doesn't involve its own difficulties, for example those concerning the difference between primary and secondary qualities. As a model for self-understanding, however, perception makes thought certain in the sense that it can be empirically measured, or observed, and hence freed from speculative or, in the sense we shall discuss, narrative complications.

26. The disturbing effect of external intrusions is a frequent theme in Coleridge, and could be considered a sign of his "empiricism." We might consider in this light, for example, the prefatory remarks to "Kubla Khan." Christensen has discussed the notion of "interruption" in Hartley and Coleridge in the second chapter of his *Coleridge's Blessed Machine of Language*.

27. It may appear rather haphazard to pass from the opening discussions of the sources of ideas to the remarks on association, since in between is the entire treatment of the actual ideas themselves, including those of the faculties that manipulate them. Following the chapter "Of Ideas in General" are extended discussions of the origin and composition of "simple" and "complex" ideas of sensation and reflection (such as color and power, duration, relation, and so on), as well as of the processes or "powers" of reason which are responsible for manipulating these ideas (such as comparing, compounding, remembering, and so on). These chapters, however, remain within the general framework established in the discussions of sensation and reflection; in the chapter on association, as we have said, we encounter an argument that seems in certain ways to come up against this framework and to struggle with it. It is in this struggle that we can learn most about how the narrative displacements are peculiar to the empirical argument of the *Essay*, and what such a fictional nonfiction is telling us.

28. See the 1805 version of Wordsworth's *Prelude*, lines 237ff. It is interesting that madness is described in Locke's definition as a disruption of what is normally a purely cognitive activity, the act of reasoning, by another sort of experience, and this distinguishes madness from mere falsehood. As the passage indicates, the most prominent feature of the experience is the loss of control over ideas which seem to take on a power of their own; when Locke goes on to connect the madness with "sympathies" and "antipathies," he implies that the loss of control is often experienced as affect. This account of the "pas-

sions" is indeed far more convincing than the discussion of them in the chapter "Of Modes of Pleasure and Pain." The madness is thus neither a rational experience nor an ordinary feeling of "passion," but an entirely different experience in which the two are somehow confused. It is an experience, that is, which puts into question the very notion of experience as it has been defined in the *Essay.*

29. See Tuveson, *The Imagination as a Means of Grace,* pp. 34–35.

30. Forced reception could really be called a Lockean topos. Note, for example, the familiarity of this hypothetical situation, offered in the chapter "Of Power" to prove that freedom is an attribute of a person and not of the will:

> Again, suppose a Man be carried, whilst fast asleep, into a Room, where is a Person he longs to see and speak with; and be there locked fast in, beyond his Power to get out: he awakes, and is glad to find himself in so desirable Company, which he stays willingly in, *i.e.* preferrs his stay to going away. I ask, Is not this stay voluntary? I think, no Body will doubt it: and yet being locked fast in, 'tis evident he is not at liberty not to stay, he has not freedom to be gone. So that *Liberty is not an* Idea *belonging to Volition,* or preferring; but to the Person Having the Power of doing, or forbearing to do. (II.21.10)

It is interesting that this scenario, which keeps reappearing in Locke's personification of the understanding, occurs in an argument against personification. We might also note that it is precisely the possibility of *will,* and not a person, that is not free, that is suggested by the association chapter.

With regard to the change from analysis to narrative, section II.33.8 explicitly turns away from distinguishing between false and true connections, claiming that the real purpose of the chapter is to help educators "prevent the undue Connexion of *Ideas*" in children. It might prove interesting to study Locke's work on education in the context of the rhetorical function, in this chapter, of the turn to the "practical."

31. In this sense the sort of self-division in association is like the rhetorically manipulative orator and audience. Harold Bloom has suggested that after its "fall" classical rhetoric surreptitiously reappears in the guise of associationism, to be transformed by the Romantics and later psychologists such as Mill and finally picked up by Freud in his theory of defense. See "Coda: Poetic Crossings," in his *Wallace Stevens: The Poems of Our Climate* (Ithaca: Cornell University Press, 1977). If the eighteenth-century theories of rational association by similarity, contiguity, and contrast reformulate the *tropes* of metaphor and metonymy, Locke's irrational association emphasizes rhetoric as

persuasion. Freud's concept of defense as a fiction with repressive purposes is in many ways closer to Locke's understanding of association than the later versions of it, although one would not want to separate too strictly the Lockean and non-Lockean versions.

32. These phrases occur in sections 7 and 15, respectively.

33. See for example II.23.2.

34. The role of "accident" in Locke's empiricism might be an interesting context in which to examine the literature of "accidents" in the eighteenth century, as well as the topos of the *sortes biblicae* (in Defoe, for example) in connection with a sort of accidental conversion. A rereading of Defoe's works, which helps overcome the frequent reduction of his narratives through an unquestioned empiricism, is to be found in David Marshall, *The Figure of Theater: Shaftesbury, Defoe, Adam Smith, and George Eliot* (New York: Columbia University Press, 1986).

35. We might sense a connection here between Locke's argument that madness is always an accident, and the implicit suggestion of Freud that there are no accidents.

36. For excellent discussions of the significance of the philosophical and literary uses of this rhetorical figure see Andrzej Warminski, *Readings in Interpretation: Hölderlin, Hegel, Heidegger* (Minneapolis: University of Minnesota Press, 1987); see also the introduction to this book by Rodolphe Gasché, "Reading Chiasms."

37. This means, specifically, for the empirical argument, that its claim to be a transparent self-reflection of "understanding" is a figurative displacement of the actual way in which understanding, in the argument, comes to know itself: as a text.

38. See Freud's essay "Mourning and Melancholia."

39. Death, as it were, passes itself off as her own kin.

40. For an excellent discussion of prosopopoeia see Cynthia Chase, "Giving a Face to a Name," in *Decomposing Figures: Rhetorical Readings in the Romantic Tradition* (Baltimore: Johns Hopkins University Press, 1986). Barbara Johnson provides perceptive remarks on a figure related to prosopopoeia, apostrophe, specifically in the context of giving faces to dead or absent children, in "Apostrophe, Animation, Abortion," in *A World of Difference* (Baltimore: Johns Hopkins University Press, 1987).

41. On the role of catachresis in philosophy see Jacques Derrida, "La mythologie blanche," in *Marges de la philosophie* (Paris: Editions de Minuit, 1972).

42. It is important to keep in mind that "figure," used in the context of the mourning passage, does not mean "fiction," but rather designates the indirectness of reference.

A consideration of Locke's book *on* language would naturally be important for a more extended reading of Locke. In particular one might note the immediate passage from the chapter on association to the discussion of the arbitrariness of the "connexions" between words and ideas. We would then have to put the entire second book in the context of the third, much as we have attempted to place the earlier chapters of the second book in the context of the chapter on association; one notices right off an interesting parallel between the movement from "simple ideas" to "association," and the movement from "the names of simple ideas" to "the abuse of words."

43. We could perhaps also think of certain philosophical traditions in terms of their ruling figures; for example the role of "force" in Kant (discussed in chapter 3) might prove to be a "reading" of the role of "motion" and "light" in Locke.

2 Past Recognition: Narrative Origins in Wordsworth and Freud

1. A somewhat shorter version of this chapter was originally presented at a panel of the 1984 MLA Convention entitled "The Romantic Ego." A highly sophisticated analysis of romantic authors through a psychoanalytic vocabulary can be found in Thomas Weiskel, *The Romantic Sublime: Studies in the Structure and Psychology of Transcendence* (Baltimore: Johns Hopkins University Press, 1976).

2. Jeffrey Mehlman, trans., *Life and Death in Psychoanalysis*, by Jean Laplanche (Baltimore: Johns Hopkins University Press, 1976), pp. 15 ff. Strictly speaking, Mehlman is translating Laplanche's translation of *Anlehnung* as *étayage*.

3. Freud distinguishes the sexual "drive" from the physical "instinct" of hunger in the *Three Essays*, referring to the former as a concept "lying on the frontier between the mental and the physical."

4. I refer here to the Blessed Babe passage proper as well as the passage following it in Book Two of *The Prelude*. Quotations of this work in the essay are from Jonathan Wordsworth, M. H. Abrams, and Stephen Gill, eds., *The Prelude, 1799, 1805, 1850,* Norton Critical Edition (New York: Norton, 1979), with edition (1805 or 1850) and line numbers provided in the text. I have chosen to quote from the 1805 version (unless otherwise noted) because the alterations in the 1850 version of the Blessed Babe passage and the one immediately succeeding it eliminate interesting material. What they add, however, is also interesting, and is treated toward the end of the essay. See note 20 for a brief discussion of difficulties in determining certain details of the 1805 version.

5. Sigmund Freud, *Three Essays on Sexuality*, trans. James Stra-

chey, *The Standard Edition of the Complete Psychological Works of Sigmund Freud*, vol. 7 (London: Hogarth Press, 1953), p. 228. Hereafter cited as S. E. 7. German text is supplied from the *Studienausgabe*, vol. 5 (Frankfurt am Main: Fischer Taschenbuch Verlag, 1982).

    6. S.E. 7, p. 222.

    7. S.E. 7, p. 182, with modifications in translation (in brackets) from *Life and Death in Psychoanalysis*, p. 18.

    8. Harold Bloom, "Wrestling Sigmund: Three Paradigms for Poetic Originality," in *The Breaking of the Vessels* (Chicago: University of Chicago Press, 1982), p. 69; cf. Laplanche, *Life and Death in Psychoanalysis*, p. 22.

    9. The connection with associationism is particularly clear in Freud's early work, *On Aphasia* (not included in the Standard Edition, but available in English translation as *On Aphasia: A Critical Study*, trans. E. Stengel (New York: International Universities Press, 1953).

    10. See David Hartley, *Observations on Man*, 2 vols., 1749. On motion in Wordsworth see Milton Wilson, "Bodies in Motion: Wordsworth's Myths of Natural Philosophy," in Eleanor Cook et al., eds., *Centre and Labyrinth: Essays in Honour of Northrop Frye* (Toronto: University of Toronto Press, 1983).

    11. The close relation between associationism and classical rhetoric is proposed by Harold Bloom in "Coda: Poetic Crossings," in his *Wallace Stevens: The Poems of Our Climate* (Ithaca: Cornell University Press, 1977), pp. 397–98. Other useful discussions of the use or interpretation of a classical rhetorical tradition and of the language of emotion are to be found in Klaus Dockhorn, "Wordsworth und die rhetorische Tradition in England," in *Macht und Wirkung der Rhetorik: Vier Ansätze zur Ideengeschichte der Vormoderne* (Berlin: Verlag Gehlen, 1968), and Josephine Miles, *Wordsworth and the Vocabulary of Emotion* (Berkeley: University of California Press, 1942).

    12. This could be written as follows:

$$\frac{\text{Poetic "Eye"}}{\text{Babe}} \times \frac{\text{Babe}}{\text{Mother's Eye}}$$

    13. Geoffrey Hartman notes the peculiarity of this passage and offers an interesting reading of it in "A Touching Compulsion: Wordsworth and the Problem of Literary Representation," *Georgia Review* 31 (1977).

    14. Another pattern evoking a "no no" is discussed by Cynthia Chase in Accidents of Disfiguration: Limits to Literal and Rhetorical Reading in Book V of *The Prelude*," *Studies in Romanticism* 18 (1979).

15. I quote from the 1850 version here because it develops some of the implicit figurative connections between passages in the 1805 version. This does not assume, however, that the versions can simply be exchanged for one another as if they were the same poem; see the discussion below on some of the differences between the versions. A helpful analysis of the relation between the boat passages in Books Four and Five is to be found in Susan Wolfson, "Wordsworth's Revisions of 'The Drowned Man of Esthwaite,'" *PMLA* 99 (October 1984).

16. See the passages beginning at (1805) IV.400ff. and (1805) V.595ff. The final appearance of props in *The Prelude* is to be found in the "Vaudracour and Julia" episode in Book Nine of the 1805 version only (ll. 453ff.). I have offered a reading of this episode in "'Unknown Causes': Poetic Effects," *Diacritics* (Winter 1987).

17. For a fine analysis of the Blind Man passage see Geraldine Friedman, "History in the Background of Wordsworth's Blind Beggar," *ELH* 56 (Spring 1989).

18. Leslie Brisman writes that the lines that end this passage "conclude the strongest dismissal of hunting for nonmythic origins, and . . . introduce the great myth of romantic origins." I would add that the movement from one passage to the next also involves a complication of this difference. See his *Romantic Origins* (Ithaca: Cornell University Press, 1978), p. 303. It might also be of interest to consider the analysis of the relation between Locke and Hartley, or of the development of "empiricism," made possible by Wordsworth's poem. (One could for example develop a reading of Locke, through Wordsworth's narrative of the mother and babe, which would pose a counterpoint to some of the later empiricist interpretations, or reductions, of Locke's work.)

19. The difference between an original version and an edition is not clear-cut in Wordsworth. Note 20 discusses this problem further.

20. De Selincourt's edition differs from the Norton Critical Edition in placing the exclamation points in the 1805 version as well as the 1850 version; it also makes some other changes in punctuation, and capitalizes *mother* and *babe* (see Ernest de Selincourt, ed., *The Prelude, or, Growth of a Poet's Mind*, new edition corrected by Stephen Gill (Oxford: Oxford University Press, 1970). Both are apparently following Manuscript A, but the editors of the Norton edition point out that punctuation and some capitalization in the 1805 manuscripts is "editorial." They also note, however, that "punctuation in the manuscripts is so spasmodic that its absence tells us nothing. Wordsworth seems not to have believed that his poetry could be misread (for instance,

asking Humphrey Davy, whom he had never met, to correct the punctuation of *Lyrical Ballads* 1800" (p. 511). This poses an interesting problem for reading the texts, since in order to decide which punctuation to choose, or to decide that any single punctuation can't be chosen, one has to shift attention from the story "in" the text to the story "of" the text, that is, the story of its manuscripts and their alterations. The exclamation points thus introduce in another way an element not entirely subordinated to the meaning of the narrative. Thus, also, the elimination of "gather" in the 1850 version does not eliminate the general problem, since in order to tell the difference between "Doth gather passion from his mother's eye" (1805) and "Drinks in the feelings of his Mother's eye!" (1850) one has to tell the story of the manuscripts.

21. It should be emphasized that these "conditions of possibility" are not *transcendental*, just as they are nonempirical; it is in the odd sense of nonempirical, nontranscendental conditions of possibility that syntax and punctuation disturb the "affective" story. For a discussion of syntax and semantics in *The Prelude* see Andrzej Warminski, "Missed Crossing: Wordsworth's Apocalypses," *MLN* 99 (December 1984).

22. Paul de Man suggests a reading of the Blessed Babe passage which focuses on the "claim" to "manifest kindred," which, he points out, is verbal and thus "not given in the nature of things." See "Wordsworth and the Victorians," in Paul de Man, *The Rhetoric of Romanticism* (New York: Columbia University Press, 1984), Cynthia Chase's discussion of the de Man text in "Giving a Face to a Name," *Decomposing Figures* (Baltimore: Johns Hopkins University Press, 1986), and Andrzej Warminski, "First Poetic Spirits," in *Diacritics* (Winter 1987).

23. Frances Ferguson suggests that the "mute dialogues" are to be understood as carrying with them "the constant affirmation of ocular and tangible proof." My analysis suggests a rereading of the ocular and tangible in terms of the nonperceptual conditions of possibility of meaning in the Blessed Babe passage. See Frances Ferguson, *Wordsworth: Language as Counter-Spirit* (New Haven: Yale University Press, 1977). Richard J. Onorato, in *The Character of the Poet: Wordsworth in "The Prelude"* (Princeton: Princeton University Press, 1971), proposes an interpretation similar to Ferguson's by reading the "mute dialogues" as a "metaphor" for the "unlimited sensation and fantasy" of the prelinguistic infant in the presence of its mother. The interpretation of the passage in terms of a prelinguistic stage of infancy subordinates language to a nonverbal experience of the presence and absence of the mother, generally understanding language empirically

as actual speaking and writing, which is derivative of, or inadequate to, a more fundamental "passion." Wordsworth's text, however, resists an empirical interpretation of language and suggests (1) that, if the narrative is interpreted as a history of development, the child is from the beginning "reading," and (2) that the narrative is not limited to its reference to such a history, and that the "gathering" of "passion" and the "removal" of the "props" do not concern a physical mother and an experienced relation to her presence and absence.

3 The Force of Example: Kant's Symbols

1. Representative of this current trend, among other critics, are Gerald Graff, in *Literature against Itself: Literary Ideas in Modern Society* (Chicago: University of Chicago Press, 1979), Frank Lentricchia, in *After the New Criticism* (Chicago: University of Chicago Press, 1980), and Edward W. Said, in *The World, the Text, and the Critic* (Cambridge: Harvard University Press, 1983).

2. Kant would not characterize Newtonian science as entirely nondiscursive; what is significant is the relation to a science that is at least in part dependent on what is materially "given" (see the discussion later in this chapter of *The Metaphysical Foundation of Natural Science* and note 15, below). Readers of Kant have had difficulty with the nature of the relation to Newtonian science; this is briefly discussed below.

3. Immanuel Kant, *Critique of Pure Reason*, trans. Norman Kemp Smith (New York: St. Martin's Press, 1965), pp. 20–21 (B xiii–xiv). References to the first *Critique* are to this edition. The preface to the second edition to this work will be referred to as the "second preface."

4. *Critique*, p. 21 (B xiv–xv).

5. Although other scientists before Newton did support the Copernican view, it was Newton's inverse square law (the law of gravitation) which reduced the complicated motion of the planets described by Ptolemy and later Copernicus to a single elegant law.

6. For a discussion of this issue see Gerd Buchdahl, "Gravity and Intelligibility: Newton to Kant," in *The Methodological Heritage of Newton*, ed. Robert E. Butts and John W. Davis (Toronto: University of Toronto Press, 1970). It should be noted that such a problem was recognized by Newton himself; and that the distinction between "science" and "philosophy" was not firmly established at this time, although it perhaps developed, in part, around this very issue. On Kant's early concern with force and the debates surrounding this

topic, see Irving I. Polonoff, *Force, Cosmos, Monads, and Other Themes of Kant's Early Thought*, in *Kantstudien*, Ergänzungshefte, 197 (Bonn: Bouvier Verlag Herbert Grundmann, 1973).

7. *Critique*, p. 585 (A 727, B 755), translation modified.

8. Ibid, p. 24 (B xix).

9. A general discussion of this distinction can be found in the second preface, pp. 27ff.

10. This is discussed in detail below.

11. This is the "theoretical" part of the system, concerned with the realm of "nature"; the place of the other part of the system, concerned with "freedom," is discussed briefly below.

12. Gerd Buchdahl, "The Kantian 'Dynamic of Reason,' with Special Reference to the Place of Causality in Kant's System," in *Kant Studies Today*, ed. Lewis White Beck (La Salle, Ill.: Open Court, 1969), p. 372, and "Kant: From Metaphysics to Transcendental Logic," in his *Metaphysics and the Philosophy of Science: The Classical Origins, Descartes to Kant* (Oxford: Basil Blackwell, 1969). See also Gordan G. Brittan, Jr., *Kant's Theory of Science* (Princeton: Princeton University Press, 1978).

13. This would be the case also for the famous "Copernican Analogy" in the second preface, along with the footnote on Newton which follows it some pages later. Interesting treatments of the analogy can be found in Hans Blumenberg, "Was ist an Kants Wendung das Kopernikanische?" in *Die Genesis der kopernikanischen Welt* (Frankfurt am Main: Suhrkamp, 1975), and in the debate between F. L. Paton, "Kant's So-called Copernican Revolution,'" and F. L. Cross, "Professor Paton and 'Kant's So-Called Copernican Revolution,'" in *Mind* 46 (1937); a more recent discussion can be found in I. Bernard Cohen, "Kant's Alleged Copernican Revolution," in *Revolution in Science* (Cambridge: Harvard University Press, 1985). The power of this model is so strong, indeed, that the *Critique of Judgment*, which is meant to bridge the "gap" between the theoretical and practical realms, is also divided in the same manner: between aesthetic and teleological judgment, in aesthetic judgment between the beautiful and the sublime, and in the sublime between the "mathematical" and the "dynamical" sublime. On the laws of force and motion as more-than-ordinary examples see Paul de Man, "Phenomenality and Materiality in Kant," in *Hermeneutics: Questions and Prospects,* ed. Gary Shapiro and Alan Sica (Amherst: University of Massachusetts Press, 1984). Helpful discussions of the architectonic which focus on the place of causality within it can be found in Gordan G. Brittan, Jr., "Kant, Closure, and Causality," in William L. Harper and Rolf Meerbote, eds., *Kant on Causality, Freedom, and Objectivity* (Minneapolis: University of Min-

nesota Press, 1984); Gerd Buchdahl, "The Relation between 'Understanding' and 'Reason' in the Architectonic of Kant's Philosophy," *Proceedings of the Aristotelian Society,* New Series, 67 (1967); A. C. Ewing, *Kant's Treatment of Causality* (London: Kegan Paul, 1924); and Sueo Takeda, *Kant und das Problem der Analogie: Eine Forschung nach dem Logos der kantischen Philosophie* (Den Haag: Martinus Jijhoff, 1969).

14. Immanuel Kant, *Metaphysical Foundations of Natural Science,* trans. James W. Ellington, in *Immanuel Kant: Philosophy of Material Nature* (Indianapolis: Hackett Publishing, 1985), p. 16; translation modified, and German words in brackets added (here and in later quotations) for purposes of clarity. Citations of the *Foundations* will be taken from this edition.

15. This passage has been a focus of much debate, since Kant is concerned in his critical philosophy with establishing a complex relation between transcendental conditions and metaphysics which would not normally be considered reducible to an opposition between form and content. It is of all the more interest, then, that the passage seems to suggest such an opposition, and thus demands a reading that does not simply dismiss or embrace it in the pre-established terms of the system. On the debate concerning this passage see Hansgeorg Hoppe, *Kants Theorie der Physik: eine Untersuchung über das Opus postumum von Kant* (Frankfurt am Main: Vittorio Klostermann, 1969).

16. *Foundations,* pp. 13−14.

17. Ibid., p. 21.

18. Ibid., pp. 104−5.

19. Newton's first law is translated by Motte as follows: "Every body continues in its state of rest, or of uniform motion in a right line, unless it is compelled to change that state by forces impressed upon it." See Sir Isaac Newton, *Principia,* vol. 1, Motte's translation, revised by Florian Cajori (Berkeley: University of California Press, 1934), p. 1. It is important to note here the difference between "external senses" as a physiological concept and the other uses of *external* in Kant's passage.

20. *Foundations,* pp. 105−6.

21. A similar shift can be found in the *Critique of Judgment,* in the movement to the "dynamical sublime," which begins with the word *power* where one might expect *force.* On this particular shift see Paul de Man, "Phenomenality and Materiality in Kant."

22. It is thus interesting that "examples" are also called, in the preface to the *Foundations,* "*Fälle* in concreto."

23. The problem of force in relation to difficulties of closure within the system as a whole is indicated by the last work of Kant, left as a series of fragments at his death, entitled *Transition from the Meta-*

physical Foundations of Natural Science to Physics. This work is concerned with the inadequacy of the *Foundations* to provide a full transition between transcendental concepts and empirical law, leaving open the possibility of a "leap" (*Sprung*) within the system. The *Transition* finally hypothesizes an aether to account for force, an odd solution, since this is presumably the sort of hypothesis that criticism is meant to avoid. The language of the justification is particularly interesting: "Without such a principle of the continual excitement of the material world there would be a deathly stillness [*die Todesruhe*] of elastic forces . . . and a complete standstill of moving forces." Here, it is force itself that is threatened by a death. See Immanuel Kant, *Gesammelte Schriften* (Berlin: Georg Reimer, 1904), vols. 21, 22, *Kants handschriftliche Nachlass*, esp. 21.310.19. Good recent work on the *Transition* can be found in Eckart Förster, ed., *Kant's Transcendental Deductions: The Three "Critiques" and the "Opus postumum"* (Stanford: Stanford University Press, 1989).

24. Immanuel Kant, *Prolegomena to Any Future Metaphysics*, trans. Lewis White Beck, Library of Liberal Arts (New York: Liberal Arts Press, 1950), pp. 96–97. Quotations of the *Prolegomena* are taken from this edition. German is supplied from the *Philosophische Bibliothek* edition, ed. Karl Vorländer (Hamburg: Felix Meiner, 1976).

25. *Prolegomena*, pp. 99–103, translation modified: *Grenzen* is translated as "limits," *Schranken* as "boundaries." The word *concepts* in the last line refers here strictly speaking to the ideas of "thinking" rather than the concepts of "knowing."

26. *Prolegomena*, pp. 105–6. "Confine" is *einschränken* in the German text.

27. Ibid., p. 106.

28. Ibid., p. 106, n. 1.

29. Immanuel Kant, *Religion within the Limits of Reason Alone*, trans. T. M. Greene and H. H. Hudson (New York: Harper & Row, 1960), p. 58.

30. It would be worth exploring the relation between the sacrificial figure in the discussion of the symbol and the characterization of the sublime in the *Critique of Judgment*.

31. John 3:16–17, King James version.

32. The place of Christ in these examples has implications for the traditional understanding of the Christ story as a meaningful redemption of Abraham's sacrifice. Kierkegaard's version of the Abraham story in *Fear and Trembling* is relevant in this context. For a reading of Kierkegaard see Kevin Newmark, "Between Hegel and Kierkegaard: The Space of Translation," *Genre* 16 (Winter 1983).

33. One might need also to reread the relation to "Hume" in the argument that defines the symbolic anthropomorphism as "not" a negation. What exactly is the status of this "not"? This would lead as well to a reconsideration of the role of "error" in general in the understanding of the "ideas": unlike empirical concepts, the ideas are first "given" not from something outside of reason (sensible or supersensible) but in error, i.e., the texts of previous metaphysics. The relation between knowing and thinking is thus not just a difference between a relation to the sensible and the supersensible, but between a relation to the sensible and to texts.

34. A full development of our reinterpretation of the metaphysical example would entail an examination of Kant's notion of "intuition" (*Anschaaung*), which is the form in which the material world is given to thought. In this context, Jaako Hinktikka's work on intuition deserves further attention. He suggests that "intuition" in Kant is not, as is generally interpreted, a kind of raw sensation, but is rather to be understood in terms of Kant's understanding of the Euclidean proof, in which the "construction of intuitions" is the diagram drawn by the mathematician to represent the geometrical object being studied. This object is also an example (thus "triangle ABC" is said to represent all isosceles triangles, and so on). Intuition would then be a matter of drawn lines and of an exemplary structure established by the claim that a particular drawn figure stands for all such figures. See Jaako Hintikka, "Kantian Intuitions," *Inquiry* 15 (1972).

35. On the traditional difficulties of linking the verbal and nonverbal sciences see Paul de Man, "The Resistance to Theory," in his *The Resistance to Theory* (Minneapolis: University of Minnesota Press, 1986). An indirectly related argument that is useful for a reading of Kant can be found in his essay "The Epistemology of Metaphor," in Sheldon Sacks, ed., *On Metaphor* (Chicago: University of Chicago Press, 1978). An excellent reading of the problematics of example in another part of Kant's system is to be found in J. Hillis Miller, "Reading Telling: Kant," in *The Ethics of Reading* (New York: Columbia University Press, 1987).

36. I put the word *linguistic* in quotation marks as a reminder that I am no longer using this term in a mere opposition to the empirical, but rather in relation to an event that cannot be thought strictly within such oppositions.

37. Can we not hear in Kant's claim in the "Doctrine of Method" (quoted above) that philosophy and mathematics "go hand in hand" (also in the German text) this very love story?

4 Signs of Love

1. Lionel Trilling, "The Authentic Unconscious," in *Sincerity and Authenticity* (Cambridge: Harvard University Press, 1972), p. 157. The precise wording of his discussion of the imperative is given in the quotation below.

2. Ibid., p. 154.

3. Trilling is ascribing to Freud a kind of negative knowledge characteristic of Kantian and post-Kantian philosophy, in which the error of a belief in truths external to thought was analyzed in terms of the structures internal to thought.

4. Trilling, "The Authentic Unconscious," pp. 157–58.

5. The argument thus takes the form of the rhetorical figure "chiasmus," a crossing or exchange between properties aligned in an inverted analogy. It is a figure fundamental to the philosophy of the aesthetic, and, in Trilling's case, makes possible the unproblematic passage between language and the world. The essay that follows could be considered a reading of this figure, upon which the aesthetic interpretation of Freud's text is founded.

6. A good discussion of the structuralist reading of Freud can be found in Jonathan Culler, *The Pursuit of Signs: Semiotics, Literature, Deconstruction* (Ithaca: Cornell University Press, 1981), chap. 9.

7. Leo Bersani, "Theory and Violence," in his *The Freudian Body: Psychoanalysis and Art* (New York: Columbia University Press, 1986), pp. 12–13.

8. Ibid., p. 21.

9. Freud discusses the oceanic feeling in chapter 1 of *Civilization*. He attributes the concept to Romain Rolland, who has argued that Freud's earlier work, *The Future of an Illusion*, does not account for a feeling of oneness with the universe which might be considered the origin of religion. Freud's critique of Romain Rolland indirectly suggests that such feelings may be masks of narcissistic aggression. See the discussion of chapter 1 below and note 26.

10. Jacques Lacan, "L'Amour du prochain," in *Le Séminaire*, vol. 7: *L'éthique de la psychanalyse* (Paris: Editions du Seuil, 1986).

11. Sigmund Freud, *Civilization and Its Discontents*, trans. James Strachey, The Standard Edition of the Complete Psychological Works of Sigmund Freud, vol. 21 (Hogarth Press, 1961), p. 131. All references to the English translation of *Civilization* refer to this edition; page numbers are cited in the text. German quotations of *Civilization* are from the *Studienausgabe*, vol. 9 (Frankfurt am Main: Fischer Taschenbuch Verlag, 1982).

12. It is on the etymological basis of this double meaning that

Nietzsche carries out his analysis of guilt in the second essay of *The Genealogy of Morals*, a work that shows interesting parallels to the critical strategy of Freud's argument. On Freud and Nietzsche see Lorin Anderson, "Freud, Nietzsche," *Salmagundi* 47–48 (1980), and Peter L. Rudnytsky, "Nietzsche," in his *Freud and Oedipus* (New York: Cornell University Press, 1987).

13. The word also occurs, in a pun, in the quotation of Goethe at the end of chapter 6 of *Civilization*. For an intriguing reading of these lines as they appear elsewhere in Freud, see Avital Ronell, *Dictations: On Haunted Writing* (Bloomington: Indiana University Press, 1986). While "guilty" is not a clearly intended meaning in the passage in chapter 7, the context in which it occurs (an accusation against the author of *Civilization*), as well as the issues raised in the work as a whole (which are discussed below), support our reading of a play on words in this passage.

14. The German phrase *feierlich auftretend* underscores the dramatic character of this argument; *auftreten* is used as a theatrical term meaning "to make one's appearance on the scene." The theatrical terminology is also present in chapter 1. I use *narcissistic* here, as later in the chapter, not in its strictly clinical sense but in its broader theoretical meaning.

15. Jacques Lacan, *L'Éthique de la psychanalyse*, p. 218.

16. The possibility, raised by the command, that all reference may be ultimately an effect of self-signifying categories is closely related to problems of "deixis," or words (such as *here* and *now* or *I*) which seem to have the most particular referents but turn out to signify the most general categories. The problem had arisen already in German philosophy in Hegel; the problem of language was thus central to the philosophical tradition (and did not arise suddenly, say, with twentieth-century structuralism). For a reading of Hegel's analysis of deixis and its relation to structuralist issues see Paul de Man, "Hypogram and Inscription," in his *The Resistance to Theory* (Minneapolis: University of Minnesota Press, 1986); see also Cynthia Chase's "Translating Romanticism," *Textual Practice* 4:3 (1990). Paul de Man discusses Hegel's analysis of the deictic in the pronoun *I* in "Sign and Symbol in Hegel's *Aesthetics*," *Critical Inquiry* 8:4 (Summer 1982).

17. This is precisely the theory of the death drive as it is discussed in *Beyond the Pleasure Principle*. The sense that we are implicitly dealing with the operation of the death drive in chapter 5 is confirmed when we discover its explicit introduction in chapter 6.

18. In chapter 7 Freud specifically refers to the aggressivity of the child as "revengeful aggressiveness" (*rachsüchtige Agression*). Thomas Keenan's conversations on revenge have been illuminating.

19. The psychoanalytic critique of the "illusion" thus operates as a reversal of the temporal scheme implied in the imperative. On a similar demystifying strategy in Nietzsche, see Paul de Man, *Allegories of Reading: Figural Language in Rousseau, Nietzsche, Rilke, and Proust* (New Haven: Yale University Press, 1979), chap. 6.

20. The centrality of the principle of reversal in the argument again emphasizes Freud's link with Kantian and post-Kantian philosophy, beginning with Kant's famous "Copernican Analogy." The figure of inversion is the figure of critical method because it reflects the fact that the "truth" of the theory is first of all its relation to a previous error, i.e., is a kind of interpretation, rather than a direct reference to the world. And this is connected with a particular insight into the problem of reference, the impossibility that a discursive theory can ever stand completely outside of the object of its knowledge. In Freud, the reversal is always asymmetrical, which could be considered a kind of critique of the critical method itself. On the figure of reversal in philosophy and literature see Werner Hamacher, "The Second Inversion: Movements of a Figure through Celan's Poetry," *Yale French Studies* 69 (1985).

21. Freud says, a page later, that "the severity of the super-ego which a child develops in no way corresponds to the severity of the treatment which he has himself met with. The severity of the form seems to be independent (*unabhängig*) of the latter" (130). He modifies this radical statement of his position in the next lines and suggests that the actual severity of the upbringing does "exert some influence" on the formation of the superego. The wavering in positions is significant, because it reflects an insight about figuration that is related to the reappearance of the third narrative, in which reference returns in a somewhat altered form. Here, it is implied (particularly in the sense of a vague, subject-less prohibition "imposed from without," a sort of force not exactly linked to an empirical world) that the act of denial is not unified, as the act of an agent, but already divided by the otherness that compels the appearance of the third narrative.

22. Much of the description of this origin of the superego, as a kind of reaction without a previous action, is reminiscent of the discussion of the death drive in *Beyond the Pleasure Principle*. The prohibition "imposed from without" is much like the "impact of external stimuli" described in that work (in chapter 4), which sets off the reaction that is the first attempt-to-return of the death drive. These forces are no longer empirical in any sense and thus the physical model of *force* in the phrase "dynamic source" becomes a drama of a *power* exchange in the later description of the superego, in this model as a character who speaks (p. 129—with a sort of irony that recalls Friedrich

Schlegel's writings on critical method and irony, and the voice of the comic "buffo" in ironic works). We might then understand the super-ego here as the agent of the death drive, as speaking in the name of death. But such an understanding anticipates, to some extent, the appearance of the third story, in which death is introduced explicitly. The connection between the two stories which will be argued for below could be understood in terms of the way death or the "death drive" functions in each. This would also tell us much about the relation between the temporality of each, the pastness of the individual and the less comprehensible past of the past, or primal history, which is linked to the origination of meaning and can no longer be understood in empirical terms.

In regard to the shift from an empirical model (of imposed forces) to a drama of power in the individual's story, it is interesting that a similar shift can be found in Kant's critical system, in the movement from the first to the third *Critique*. The shift is an indication of the impossibility for a discursive theory to maintain the scientific or mathematically stabilized language of physics, that is, to remain outside of and in control over its object—to be a pure "meta-language." On the curious external stimuli of *Beyond the Pleasure Principle* and the problem of the divided origin, see Samuel Weber, *The Legend of Freud* (Minneapolis: University of Minnesota Press, 1982), Pt. 3, "Love Stories."

23. All three hypotheses are concerned with the impossibility of finding an object that is represented, or functions, as single and unified; they are thus implicitly concerned with the problems raised by the stories of chapter 7.

24. Can we also hear, in *richten*, the figure of critical reversal in the Copernican Analogy (*Bisher nahm man an, alle unsere Erkenntnis müsse sich nach den Gegenständen richten. . . .*)?

25. Freud's footnotes have attracted considerable attention. On the two footnotes on smell in *Civilization*, see Jane Gallop, *The Daughter's Seduction: Feminism and Psychoanalysis* (Ithaca: Cornell University Press, 1982), pp. 26 ff. A more general discussion of the significance of the footnotes is to be found in Bersani, "Theory and Violence."

26. On Rolland's place in Freud's essay, see David James Fisher, "Reading Freud's *Civilization and Its Discontents*," in *Modern European Intellectual History*, ed. Dominick La Capra and Steven L. Kaplan (Ithaca: Cornell University Press, 1982). Fisher, who interprets Rolland as Freud's literary "double," notes a link between Rolland's first name and the Rome metaphor of chapter 1, and suggests also that the French meaning of *roman* would be of significance in associating

Rolland, in Freud's mind, with literature. We might perhaps see an interesting connection as well in the appearance of the word *Roman* at the moment of theoretical self-reflection in chapter 7.

27. John Galsworthy, "The Apple Tree," in *Five Tales* (New York: Charles Scribner's Sons, 1921), p. 278. Quotations from "The Apple Tree" refer to this edition.

28. The Hebrew is דיאד נטד (Magen David). It means literally "shield of David" but, because the shield is shaped like a star, has also come to mean "star of David."

29. *Oedipal* is used here according to the more traditional psychoanalytical use of the term rather than as a direct reference to the play itself. The play, as has been sufficiently recognized, does not conclude as to the actuality of the family configuration and focuses rather on the way in which Oedipus himself comes to conclude on its certainty. The *Hippolytus* tells a story that is in some sense implicit in the other play, and is not meant to be understood here as a simple reversal of it.

30. *Euripides,* The Athenian Drama, vol. 4, trans. Gilbert Murray (New York: Longman, Green, & Co., 1904), p. 54. Quotations from the English translation of the *Hippolytus* refer to this edition. Citations of the Greek are from Euripides, *Hippolytos,* ed. W. S. Barrett (Oxford: Clarendon Press, 1904).

31. The Greek phrase is πεῖσαι φρένα, "persuaded the wits." Murray's (very Shakespearean) translation of the play elaborates interestingly on the figure of dumbness. The place and importance of translation in the story is discussed below.

32. Theseus and Hippolytus thus both depend on the figure of prosopopoeia, the giving of face or figure to the absent or dead. As in Freud's text, the necessity of figuring the dead, or allowing the dead to speak to us, becomes the central question about the way in which language works, about whether it "creates" objects the way a subject creates, or if this very conception of language as creating its referents tells us something else about the difficulties of achieving a full discursive understanding of discourse (and, likewise, of consciousness). On the significance of prosopopoeia and its relation to apostrophe see Paul de Man, "Autobiography as De-Facement," *MLN* 94:5 (December 1979), as well as "Hypogram and Inscription."

The problem of distinguishing Theseus's and Hippolytus's positions around this figure might be called a question of *deciding* (*entscheiden*), a word that appears in interesting ways in Freud's text, and ends the sentence that introduces the alternative theory of sexuality (Freud says that the truth of this hypothesis *ist schwer zu entscheiden*). It would be interesting to compare in this context Neil Hertz's notion of the "pathos of uncertain agency" (in which "a subject is conjured up—perhaps a killer, perhaps only the discoverer of the corpse—who can serve as a locus of vacillation: did I do it? Or had it already been done?) that he develops in regard to the figure of the mother in the work of Paul de Man. See "Lurid Figures," in *Reading de Man Reading*, ed. Lindsay Waters and Wlad Godzich (Minnesota: University of Minnesota Press, 1989).

33. The phrase describing the seal is τύποι σφενδόνησ χρυσηλάτου, "engravings of the golden seal." τύποι implies a notion of having been beaten or struck, of force having been applied in some manner; here we might see a link between prohibitions as stimuli "imposed from without" and the notion of "language" as a mark to be read, a mark imposed in some manner yet not an empirical mark and not by a previously constituted subject.

34. The problem of deciding between mark and sign was first brilliantly developed by Cynthia Chase in an examination of the relation between reference, signification, and figure in Freud and Lacan, which relates these to Kristeva's notion of the "abjection" of the mother (clearly of interest here). See Cynthia Chase, "The Witty Butcher's Wife: Freud, Lacan, and the Conversion of the Resistance to Theory," *MLN: Comparative Literature Issue* (December 1987).

35. The love story is indeed, from the beginning, always focused on the speaking or naming of the love rather than on the love "itself."

36. This unseen Amazon, which reminds us that the play leaves open, always, the space of another mother, means that we could never say, for example, that the mother is "just" a figure of a linguistic problem; the Amazon is like the dead *body* attached to the text or the extra bit of reference that refuses to go away.

37. The masculine form is used here with specific reference to the masculine position in the configuration staged in the text.

38. Galsworthy, *The Apple Tree*, p. 201 (epigraph).

39. Greek art has been, particularly in the German tradition, the epitome of the aesthetic, the means by which a kind of cultural self-consciousness can be achieved. The story thus provides a reading of the interpretation of literature as an aesthetic object, i.e., as something grounded in phenomenal representation. The notion of aesthetic value as our very familiar context for reading literature thus becomes linked to the problems of reference raised by these texts.

40. This is a sort of doubling of narrative, in which theory appears in its history, as the story of the appearance "on the scene" of the death drive, which is itself structured like a historical narrative (the "attempt to return" to an origin).

41. Freud, Standard Edition, vol. 19, p. 46, translation modified.

42. Ibid., p. 46.

43. On the relation of Eros and Thanatos as figurative and literal meaning, see Harold Bloom, "Freud's Concepts of Defense and the Poetic Will," in his *Agon* (New York: Oxford University Press, 1982).

44. In this context it is interesting that the words by which Freud dramatizes the self-aggression perpetrated by the superego in the story of the individual—"If I were the father, and you the child, I should treat you badly"—resemble very closely the words used by Hippolytus in confronting his father: "By my faith, wert thou / The son, and I the sire . . . I had not exiled thee . . . / But lifted once mine arm, and struck thee dead!"

45. This phrase is meant to resonate with its use in "The Witty Butcher's Wife." On the relation between reference and imperative see Werner Hamacher, "LECTIO: de Man's Imperative," in Waters and Godzich, *Reading de Man Reading*.

Conclusion: Mourning Experience

1. *Ontological Relativity and Other Essays* (New York: Columbia University Press, 1969). It is intriguing and significant that Quine has chosen to designate himself as an empiricist in spite of his critique of some elements in the empirical tradition, and in spite of the fact that one cannot simply confuse the classical English empirical tradition with modern analytic philosophy, in which Quine's thought inscribes itself. I find Quine's paradoxes evocative in the context of my own inquiry into empiricism; but where Quine remains interested, as do analytic philosophers in general, in the rational norm by which standards of meaning are established—a norm which excludes, to borrow his own words, "the blind" and "the insane"—the essays here have turned back to precisely those eccentric deviations, and have suggested that these irrational or negative elements of meaning are indeed essential and contribute integrally to the very binding of language to experience. In a somewhat opposite direction to what analytic philosophy endeavors, then, the present inquiry investigates not merely the way in which the texts under consideration finally *make sense*, but also, specifically, the way in which the texts significantly *lose* their sense, or mark areas where the border between sense and senselessness is no longer clear. It is from the perspective of this border territory that the present study has proposed to reconsider the meaning and insistence of what might be called an ineluctable empiricism.

INDEX

Printed in Poland
by Amazon Fulfillment
Poland Sp. z o.o., Wrocław

15752134R00103